DICTIONARY OF
PROVERBS

DICTIONARY OF PROVERBS

Bloomsbury Books
London

This edition published 1994 by Bloomsbury Books, an imprint of The Godfrey Cave Group, 42 Bloomsbury Street, London, WC1B 3QJ.

ISBN 1 85471 545 3

Printed and bound in France by Maury Eurolivres

CONTENTS

Age, Youth and Wisdom	7
Appearance, Conduct and Dress	24
Crime and Punishment	39
Death, Suffering and Grief	62
Enterprise and Commerce	79
Family and Friends	90
Food and Drink	112
Fools and Folly	123
Health and Happiness	144
Knowledge and Learning	153
Love and Marriage	168
Poverty and Wealth	183
Power and Conflict	206
Prudence, Caution and Excess	222
Time, Season and Weather	241

AGE, YOUTH AND WISDOM

A child among men will soon be a man.

A creaking door hangs long on its hinges.

A fence lasts three years, a dog lasts three fences, a horse three dogs, and a man three horses.

A good life keeps off wrinkles.

A growing youth has a wolf in his belly.

A lazy youth, a lousy age.

A long life hath long miseries.

A man among children will be long a child.

A man as he manages himself, may die old at thirty or young at eighty.

A man at five may be a fool at fifteen.

A man at sixteen will prove a child at sixty.

A man often admits that his memory is at fault but never his judgement.

A new net won't catch an old bird.

A prudent youth is superior to a stupid old man.

A wild colt may become a sober old horse.

A worm is in the bud of youth and at the root of old age.

A young man negligent, an old man necessitous.

A young preacher, a new hell.

Action from youth, advice from middle age, prayers from the aged.

Affectation of wisdom often prevents us from becoming wise.

Age but tastes, youth devours.

Age is a sorry travelling companion.

All of us must be drunk once, youth is drunkenness without wine.

All would live long, but none would be old.

An idle youth, a needy age.

An old cat laps as much as a young kitten.

An old dog bites sore.

An old dog cannot alter its way of barking.

An old dog does not bark for nothing.

An old dog does not grow used to the collar.

An old dog will learn no tricks.

An old fox needs no craft.

An old lion is better than a young ass.

An old man is a bed full of bones.

An old man never wants a tale to tell.

An old man's saying's are seldom untrue.

An old man's shadow is better than a young man's sword.

An old ox ploughs a straight furrow.

An old ox will find shelter for himself.

An old physician and a young lawyer are the best.

An old poacher makes the best keeper.

An old soldier, an old fool.

An unseeded youth, a needy age.

As the boy, so the man.

As the old birds sing the young ones twitter.

As the old cock crows so the young ones learn.

As we journey through life let us live by the way.

Bend the willow while it is young.

Better eat grey bread in youth than in your age.

Better poor, young, and wise, than rich, old and a fool.

Better to live well than to live long.

Better under the beard of the old man than the whip of the young.

Both folly and wisdom come upon us with years.

Boys will be boys.

Consider well and oft why thou comest into this world and how soon thou must go out of it.

Consult with the old and fence with the young.

Crabbed age and youth cannot live together.

Credulity is the man's weakness, but the child's strength.

Custom in infancy becomes nature in old age.

Don't teach your grandmother to suck eggs.

Every station in life has duties which are proper to it.

Few persons know how to be old.

Footprints in the sand of time are not made by sitting down.

Happy is he that knows his follies in his youth.

He is oft the wisest man who is not wise at all.

He is well onward in the way of wisdom, who can bear a reproof and mend by it.

He is young enough who has health, and he is rich enough who has no debts.

He lives long that lives till all are weary of him.

He lives long that lives well.

He lives longest that is awake most hours.

He that corrects not youth controls not age.

He that is not gallant at twenty, strong at thirty, rich at forty or experienced at fifty, will never be gallant, strong, rich or experienced.

He that would be long an old man must begin early to be one.

He who lives a long life must pass through much evil.

He who lives after nature shall never be poor; after opinion shall never be rich.

Heavy work in youth is quiet rest in old age.

If only youth had the knowledge; if only age had the strength.

If the old dog barks he gives counsel.

If the young knew, if the old man could, there is nothing but would be done.

If you lie upon roses while young, you'll lie upon thorns when old.

If you live enough before thirty you won't care to live at all after fifty.

If you play with boys you must take boy's play.

If youth knew what old age would crave,
It would both get and save.

In childhood be modest, in youth temperate, in manhood just, in old age, prudent.

In the short life of man, no lost time can be afforded.

In youth beauty and wisdom is but rare.

Intemperate youth ends in an age imperfect and unsound.

It has been a great misfortune to many a one that he lived too long.

It is always the season for the old to learn.

It is as well now and then not to remember all we know.

It is difficult to grow old gracefully.

It is hard to put old heads on young shoulders.

It is less painful to learn in youth than to be ignorant in age.

It is not easy to straighten in the oak the crook that grew in the sapling.

It is the common failing of old men to attribute all wisdom to themselves.

Life begins at forty.

Life is half spent before one knows what life is.

Life is not measured by the time we live.

Life is short, yet sweet.

Life is too short to learn more than one business well.

Life that is too short for the happy is too long for the miserable.

Life's but a walking shadow.

Live not for time, but eternity.

Memory tempers prosperity, mitigates adversity and controls youth and delights old age.

Men are but children of a larger growth.

Men who live to be a hundred will not die at fifty.

Most old men are like old trees, past bearing themselves, will suffer no young plants to flourish beneath them.

No age agreeable but that of a wise man.

Never too old to learn.

No fool like an old fool

No man believes his own life will be short.

No man is born wise.

No man is so old but thinks he may live another day.

No man is the worse for knowing the worst of
himself.

No one so old that he may not live a year, none so
young that he may die today.

Of all the plagues none can compare with climbing
boys.

Old age and treachery will always defeat youth and
skill.

Old age brings companions with it.

Old age comes uncalled.

Old age, though despised, is coveted by all.

Old age itself is a disease.

Old age is a troublesome guest.

Old age is honourable.

Old boys have their playthings as well as young ones;
the difference is only in price.

Old head and young hand.

Old men are twice children.

Old men for counsel, young men for war.

Old men who have loved young company have been of long life.

Old oxen have stiff horns.

Old oxen tread hard.

Old people see best in the distance.

Our time runs on like a stream, first falls the leaves and then the tree.

Reckless youth makes rueful old age.

Secure the three things, virtue, wealth and happiness, they will serve as a staff in old age.

Talents are best nurtured in solitude, but character in life's tempestuous sea.

That is pleasant to remember that which was hard to endure.

The aged in council, the young in action.

The bread of repentance we eat is often made of the wild oats we sow in our youth.

The follies of youth are food for repentance in old age.

The great man is he that does not lose his child's heart.

The great use of life is to spend it for something that outlasts it.

The longest life is but a parcel of moments.

The old effect more by counsel than the young by war.

The old for want of ability and the young for want of knowledge let things be lost.

The old forget, the young don't know.

The old have death before their face, the young behind their back.

The old have every day something new.

The old man who dances furnishes the devil fine sport.

The old man who is loved is winter with flowers.

The old man's counsel is half deed.

The old ones sing, the young ones pipe.

The old see better behind than the young before.

The oldest man that ever lived died at last.

The only jewel you can carry beyond the grave is wisdom.

The only sure path to a tranquil life is through virtue.

The remembrance of a well spent life is sweet.

The reputation of a man depends on the first steps he takes in the world.

The warnings of age are the weapons of youth.

The way to live much is to live well betimes.

The web of your life is of a mingled yarn, good and ill together.

The young are slaves to novelty, the old to custom.

The young are not always with their bows bent.

The young man's wrath is like straw of fire,
But like red hot steel is the old man's ire.

There are more lamb skins than sheep skins.

There is a difference between living long and suffering long.

There's many a good tune played on an old fiddle.

There is a learning time in youth which suffered to
escape and no foundation laid, seldom returns

They live too long who happiness outlive.

They who live longest will see most.

They who would be young when they are old must be
old when they are young.

'Tis very certain the desire of life prolongs it.

To live long it is necessary to live slowly.

True wisdom is the price of happiness.

Wanton kittens make sober cats.

We are born crying, live complaining, and die disap-
pointed.

We have all forgotten more than we remember.

We live not as we would but as we can.

We must not look for a golden life in an iron age.

We shall never be younger.

We pass our lives in doing what we ought not, and
leaving undone what we ought to.

What the old man does is always correct.

What youth learns age does not forget.

When an old dog bites look out.

When men grow old they become more foolish and more wise.

When old age is evil youth can learn no good.

When the boy is growing he has a wolf in his belly.

Where the old are foolish the child learns folly.

Who follow not virtue in youth cannot fly sin in old age.

Who honours not age is unworthy of it.

Who is lazy in their youth must work in old age.

Who lives well sees afar off.

Who lives will see.

Who would be young in age, must in youth be sage.

Who would grow old with honour must begin early.

Whosoever masters not his own life may not be master of another's.

Wisdom adorns riches and shadows poverty.

Wisdom at proper times will forget.

Wisdom goes not always by years.

Wisdom in the mind is better than money in the hand.

Wisdom is a good purchase though we pay dear for it.

Wisdom is humble that he knows no more.

Wisdom is more to be envied than riches.

Wisdom is the least burdensome travelling pack.

Wisdom is the sunlight of the soul.

Wisdom rides on the ruins of folly.

Wisdom sometimes walks in clouted shoes.

Wisdom was the daughter of Knowledge by
  Reflection.

You are only as old as you feel.

You can't teach an old dog new tricks.

You cannot catch old birds with chaff.

You may break a colt, but not an old horse.

Young folk, silly folk, old folk, cold folk.

Young man soon give and soon forget affronts, old age is slow at both.

Young men are made wise, old men become so.

Young men should be learners when old men are actors.

Young men think old men are fools, and old men know young men to be so.

Young men's knocks old men feel.

Young people must be taught, old ones be honoured.

Young saint, old devil.

Youth and age will never agree.

Youth and white paper take any impression.

Youth comes but once in a lifetime.

Youth is a blunder, manhood a struggle, old age a regret.

Youth is a garland of roses, age is a crown of thorns.

Youth is full of pleasance, old age is full of care.

Youth is merry and holds no society with grief.

Youth is life's seed time.

AGE, YOUTH AND WISDOM

Youth is the season of hope.

Youth looks forward and age backward.

Youth may stray but return at last.

Youth must be served.

Youth ne'er casts for peril.

Youth should be a saving's bank.

Youth will have it's swing.

APPEARANCE, CUSTOM AND DRESS

A bad excuse is better than none.

A barking dog never bites.

A brain is worth little without a tongue.

A civil question deserves a civil answer.

A clean glove often hides a dirty hand.

A fair face may be a foul bargain.

A fair face may hide a foul heart.

A fair face will get its praise though the owner keep silent.

A gentleman should be honest in his actions and refined in his language.

A good anvil does not fear the hammer.

A good archer is not known by his arrow but by his aim.

A good horse is never of a bad colour.

A good name is a second inheritance.

A good name keeps its lustre in the dark.

A good word is as soon said as a bad one.

A grave and majestic outside is as it were the palace of the soul.

A hog in armour is still but a hog.

A leopard cannot change it's spots.

A liar ought to have a good memory.

A loud voice bespeaks a vulgar man.

A man is not known by his looks, nor is the sea measured with a bushel.

A man never speaks of himself without loss.

A man's character reaches town before his person.

A monkey remains a monkey though dressed in silk.

A proud look makes foul work in a fair face.

A quiet tongue shows a wise head.

A silent tongue and a true heart are the most admirable things on earth.

A smart coat is a good letter of introduction.

A sober man, a soft answer.

A still tongue makes a wise head.

A straight stick is crooked in the water.

Act honestly and go boldly.

Act so in the valley so you need never fear those who stand on the hill.

Actions speak louder than words.

Affected superiority mars good fellowship.

After the land's manner is mannerly.

Ale sellers should not be tale tellers.

All are not asleep who have their eyes shut.

All cats are grey in the dark.

All doors open to courtesy.

All that glitters is not gold.

APPEARANCE, CUSTOM AND DRESS

Always appear what you are and a little below it.

An ape's an ape, a varlet's a varlet,
  Though he be dressed in silk or scarlet.

An art requires a whole man.

Appearances are deceitful.

As a man dresses so is he esteemed.

As the man so is his speech.

As you make your bed so must you lie on it.

As you sow, so you reap.

Ask advice of your equals, help of your superiors.

Ask me no questions and I'll tell you no lies.

Ask no questions and hear no lies.

Be not the trumpeter of your own praise.

Be silent or say something better than silence.

Be what you appear to be.

Bear and forebear.

Beauty and understanding seldom go together.

Beauty blemished once is forever lost.

Beauty comes not by forcing.

Beauty doth varnish age.

Beauty draws more than the oxen.

Beauty draws with a single hair.

Beauty is a frail advantage.

Beauty is in the eye of the beholder.

Beauty is no inheritance.

Beauty is but skin deep.

Beauty is the eye's food and the soul's sorrow.

Beauty is truth, truth beauty.

Beauty is worse than wine; it intoxicates both the holder and the beholder.

Beauty will buy no beef.

Beauty without modesty is infamous.

Beauty without virtue is a curse.

Better late than never.

Better to give than to receive.

Beware the wolf in sheep's clothing.

Brave actions never need a trumpet.

By nature all men are alike, but by education widely different.

By the stubble you may guess the grain.

Children should be seen and not heard.

Civility costs nothing.

Cleanliness is next to godliness.

Clothes make the man.

Compliments cost nothing, yet many pay dear for them.

Discretion is the better part of valour.

Do not always judge by appearances

Do not judge a book by it's cover.

Do not look a gift horse in the mouth.

Don't hide your light under a bushel.

Dress slowly when you are in a hurry.

Every picture tells a story.

Every rose has its thorn.

Fair play is a jewel.

Fine feathers make fine birds.

Fine linen often conceals a foul skin.

First impressions are the most lasting.

Give every man his due.

Good advice can be given, good name cannot be given.

Good looks buy nothing in the market.

Good manners are made up of petty sacrifices.

Goodness brightens beauty.

Handsome is as handsome does.

He gives double who gives unasked.

He looks as though butter would not melt in his mouth.

He that is proud of his clothes gets his reputation from his tailor.

He that is unkind to his own, will be unkind to others.

He that knows when to speak knows when to be silent too.

He who abuses others must not be particular about he answer he gets.

He who dresses in others' clothes will be undressed on the highway.

He who gives grudgingly shall be taught better by adversity.

He who has but one coat cannot lend it.

He who holds his tongue saves his head.

He who lives by the alter must serve by the alter.

He who says what he likes hears what he does not like.

If the cap fits wear it.

Imitation is the sincerest form of flattery.

In the land of the naked, people are ashamed of clothes.

In this world it is necessary that we help one another.

In your own country your name, in other countries your appearance.

It is a good tongue that speaks no ill.

It is an ill bird that fouls its own nest

It is not the fine but the course and ill-spun that breaks.

It is not the habit that makes the monk.

It is often better not to see an insult than to avenge it.

It is the quiet people who are dangerous.

It's the thought, not the action that counts.

Keep not two tongues in one mouth.

Let him mend his manners, they will be his own another day.

Let not your tongue cut your throat.

Long and lazy, little and loud, fat and fulsome, pretty and proud.

Manners and money make the gentleman.

Manners make the man.

Manners often make fortunes.

Meat is much, but manners is more.

Men seek less to be instructed than applauded.

Much is expected where much is given.

Near is my shirt, but nearer is my skin.

Nine tailors make the man.

No fine clothes can hide the clown.

No fire without smoke.

No smoke without fire.

Not every sort of wood is fit to make an arrow.

Nothing comes of nothing.

Novelty always appears handsome.

Offenders never pardon.

Old habits die hard.

One does not wash one's dirty linen in public.

One good turn deserves another.

One must be either hammer or anvil.

One never lost anything by politeness.

Other times, other manners.

Out of sight, out of mind.

Over the greatest beauty hangs the greatest pain.

Patience is a virtue.

People who live in glass houses should not throw stones.

Politeness is benevolence in small things.

Practice what you preach.

Pride goes before a fall.

Promises, like pie-crust, are made to be broken.

Proud looks lose hearts, but courteous words win them.

Punctuality and politeness are the inseparable companions of gentlemen.

Rich garments weep on unworthy shoulders.

Ruling one's anger well is not so good as preventing the anger.

Say not all you know, but believe all that you say.

See no evil, hear no evil, speak no evil.

Silence is golden.

Small is beautiful.

Spare to speak and spare to speed.

Still waters run deep.

Talk is cheap.

The archer that shoots badly has a lie ready.

The best manners are stained by the addition of pride.

The beetle is a beauty in the eyes of its mother.

The courteous learns his courtesy from the discourteous.

The cowl does not make the monk.

The eyes are the window of the soul.

The fairest rose at last is withered.

The golden covering does not make the ass a horse.

The grass is always greener on the other side.

The handsomest flower is not the sweetest.

The man in boots does not know the man in shoes.

The manner of speaking is as important as the matter.

The peacock hath fair feathers but foul feet.

The pot calls the kettle black.

The smith and his penny are both black.

The style is the man.

The tree is known by it's fruit.

The white coat does not make the miller.

There are black sheep in every flock.

There are spots even on the sun.

There is a time and a place for everything.

There is no accounting for taste.

There is no making a good cloak of bad cloth.

There is no trusting to appearances.

Think first and then speak.

Thistles and thorns prick sore, but evil tongues prick more.

Too much humility is pride.

Two things a man should never be angry at; what he can help and what he cannot.

Under a good cloak may be a bad man.

Under a shabby cloak may be a smart thinker.

Under the thorn grow the roses.

Virtue is it's own reward.

Virtue is the one and only nobility.

Vulgarity in manners defiles garments more than mud.

We may give advice but we cannot give conduct.

We seize the beautiful and reject the useful.

We should never be too proud to take advice even from the lowly.

What you see is what you get.

When angry, count ten; when very angry, a hundred.

When bowing, bow low.

When either side grows warm to argument the wisest man gives over first.

When in doubt, do nothing.

When in Rome, do as the Romans do.

When you have nothing to say, say nothing.

Where there is whispering there is lying.

Who answers for another pays.

Who answers suddenly knows little.

Who says little has little to answer for.

Whose heart is narrow his tongue is large.

You can't make a silk purse from a sow's ear.

You can't please everyone.

You can't put new wine in old bottles.

CRIME AND PUNISHMENT

A bad dog never sees the wolf.

A bad penny always comes back.

A bad tree does not yield young apples.

A crow is never the whiter for ever washing.

A fair booty makes a fair thief.

A fault confessed is half redressed.

A gold ring does not cure a felon.

A great crime is in a great man greater.

A hundred years of wrong do not make an hour of right.

A man who is his own lawyer has a fool for a client.

A mischievous dog must be tied short.

A monarch should be slow to punish, swift to reward.

A rotten egg cannot be spoiled.

A sinful heart makes a feeble hand.

A thief does not willingly see another carry a basket.

A thief is better than a lazy servant.

A thief knows a thief as a wolf knows a wolf.

A thief passes for a gentleman when stealing has made him rich.

A thief seldom grows rich by thieving.

A thief thinks every man steals.

A wolf is a wolf though it hath torn no sheep.

Accusing is proving when malice and force sit as judges.

Accusing the times is only accusing yourselves.

Advice after mischief is like medicine after death.

After one vice a greater follows.

Agree, for the law is costly.

All are not hanged who are condemned.

All are not thieves whom the dogs bark at.

All beginnings are hard, said the thief, and began by stealing the anvil.

All criminals turn preacher when under the gallows.

All fear but fear of heaven betrays a guilt.

All temptations are found in either hope or fear.

All vice infatuates and corrupts the judgement.

Although invisible there are always two witnesses present at our every action; God and our conscience.

An evil deed has a witness in the bosom.

An old physician and a young lawyer make the best counsel.

An old thief desires a new halter.

An open box tempts the thief.

Anger is to be avoided in inflicting punishment.

Anger punishes itself.

As good steal the horse as look over the hedge.

At an open chest the righteous sins.

Bad watch often feeds the wolf.

Better no law than law not enforced.

Better ten guilty escape than one innocent man suffer.

Better to be beaten than to be in bad company.

Better to do nothing than to do ill.

Birds of a feather flock together.

Bloody and deceitful men dig their own graves.

Caesar's wife must be above suspicion.

Catching is before hanging.

Charity covers a multitude of sins.

Cheats never prosper.

Commit a sin thrice and you will think it allowable.

Confession is good for the soul.

Conquer one besetting sin at a time.

Conscience makes cowards of us all.

Constant dropping wears away the stone.

Crime never pays.

Crimes may be secret, but not secure.

Criminals are punished that others may be amended.

Crooked by nature is never made straight by
education.

Crooked iron may be straightened with a hammer.

Crows are never the whiter for washing themselves.

Curiosity often brings its own punishment.

Cut off the dog's tail he remains a dog.

Deceit and treachery make no man rich.

Deceit is in haste, but honesty can wait a fair leisure.

Devils must be driven out with devils.

Do as little as you can repent of.

Don't hear one and judge two.

Even doubtful accusations leave a stain behind them.

Every herring must hang by it's own gill.

Every land has its own law.

Every sin carries its own punishment.

Every tribe has its thief, every mountain its wolf.

Everyone takes his flogging in his own way.

Everyone's censure is first moulded in his own nature.

Evil comes to fall on him that goes to seek it.

Evil doers are evil dreaders.

Evil is soon done but slowly mended.

Examples of justice are more merciful than the unbounded exercise of pity.

Extreme justice is extreme injustice.

First a turnip, then a sheep, next a cow, and then the gallows.

Give a dog a bad name and hang him.

Give him enough rope and he will hang himself.

God help the sheep when the wolf is judge.

God permits the wicked, but not forever.

Gold is the devils fish-hook.

Good men are scarce.

Great thieves always have their sleeves full of gags.

Guilt has quick ears to a confession.

Guilt is always cowardly.

Guilt is always zealous.

Guilt sinks the brave to cowards.

Guilty men still judge others like them.

Guilty men still suspect what they deserve.

Habit in sinning takes away the sense of sin.

Half the truth is often the whole lie.

Hang him that have no shift and him that hath too
   many.

Hang the young thief and the old one will not steal.

Hanging is the worst use a man can be put to.

Hard cases make the law.

He acts the third crime that defends the first.

He confesses his guilt who flies from his trial.

He declares himself guilty who justifies himself
   before accusation.

He is a thief for he has taken a cup too many.

He is a thief indeed that robs a thief.

He keeps his road well enough who gets rid of bad company.

He sins as much who holds the bag as he who puts into it.

He that deals in dirt always has dirty fingers.

He that forgives gains the victory.

He that has an ill name is half hanged.

He that is disposed for mischief will never want occasion.

He that is embarked with the devil must sail with him.

He that is foolish in the fault, let him be wise in the punishment.

He that is innocent may well be confident.

He that lies down with dogs will get up with fleas.

He that shows his wealth to a thief is the cause of his own pillage.

He that slays shall be slain.

He that spares the wicked injures the good.

He that spares vice wrongs virtue.

He that wants to beat a dog is sure to find a stick.

He that will steal a pin will steal a better thing.

He who accuses too many accuses himself.

He who denies confesses all.

He who has a son grown up should not call another a thief.

He who is free from vice himself is the slower to suspect it in others.

He who lives wickedly lives in fear.

He who makes a law should keep it.

He who profits by a crime commits it.

He who sups with the devil should have a long spoon.

He's armed without that's innocent within.

Him who errs forgive once, but never twice.

Honesty is the best policy.

Hunger drives the wolf out of the wood.

Hunt with the wolves and be hunted with the wolves.

I am a man more sinned against than sinning.

I must be cruel only to be kind.

I'll trust him no farther than I can throw a millstone.

Idleness is the root of all evil.

If a man deceive me once, shame on him, if he deceives me twice shame on me.

If there were no receiver there would be no thief.

If you are born to be hanged then you will never be drowned.

If you can't be good, be careful.

If you cut down the woods you'll catch the thief.

If you would make a thief honest trust him.

Ignorance of the law is no excuse for breaking it.

Ill doth the devil deserve his servants.

Ill-gotten goods never thrive.

Ill laying up makes many thieves.

Ill weeds grow apace.

Ill-got, ill-spent.

In the land of sinners the unjust sit in judgement.

Innocence finds not so much protection as guilt.

Innocence is a wall of brass.

Innocence is no protection.

Innocence itself sometimes hath need of a mark.

Innocent actions carry their warrants with them.

It is an ill bird that fouls its own nest.

It is better to suffer wrong than do it.

It is cruelty to the innocent not to punish the guilty.

It is easier to hurt than to heal.

It is easy robbing when the dog is quietened.

It is easy to rob an orchard when none keeps it.

It is folly to expect justice from the unprincipled.

It is hard to steal where the host himself is a thief.

It is honourable to be accused by those who deserve
to be accused.

It is less to suffer punishment than to deserve it.

It is more noble to pardon than to punish.

It is never too late to mend.

It is not enough to know how to steal, one must know how to conceal.

It is seldom that punishment, though lame of foot, has failed to overtake a villain.

It is the raised stick makes the dog obey.

It is wit to pick a lock and steal a horse, but wisdom to leave it alone.

Judge not that you be not judged.

Justice was never angry.

Keep yourself from opportunity and God will keep you from sin.

Know how to deceive, do not deceive.

Late repentance is seldom worth much.

Law cannot persuade where it cannot punish.

Law catches flies and lets hornets go free.

Law makers should not be law breakers

Laws go the way kings direct.

Laws grind the poor, and rich men rule the law.

Laws were made for rogues.

Laws were made to be broken.

Let justice be done or the heavens fall.

Let the punishment fit the crime.

Let them who deserve their punishment bear it patiently.

Little thieves are hanged by the neck, and great thieves by the purse.

Locks and keys are not made for honest fingers.

Look not at the thieves eating flesh, but look at them suffering punishment.

Man hath no greater enemy than himself.

Man punishes the action, but God the intention.

Many without punishment, none without sin.

Men are never so easily deceived as when they are trying to deceive others.

Money and friendship bribe justice.

Murder will out.

Necessity knows no law.

Needs must when the devil drives.

Never do evil that good may come of it.

New lords, new laws.

Nip sin in the bud.

No armour is proof against the gallows.

No crime is more infamous than the violation of the truth

No deceit like the world's.

No man may be both accuser and judge.

No one likes justice brought home to his own door.

No one should be judge in his own case.

No villain like the conscientious villain.

Nothing is law that is not reason.

Nothing is profitable which is dishonest.

Old sin, new shame.

Old sins cast long shadows.

Once a rogue, always a rogue.

One crime has to be concealed by another.

One deceit brings on another.

One law for the rich and another for the poor.

One might as well be hanged for a sheep as a lamb.

One rotten apple in the barrel infects the rest.

One wrong step may give you great fall.

Opportunity makes the thief.

Our desires may undo us.

Plenty of words when the cause is lost.

Poverty is not a crime.

Prevention is better than cure.

Put a miller, a weaver, and a tailor in a bag and shake them, the first that comes out will be a thief.

Revenge is a kind of wild justice.

Revenge is sweet.

Riches without law are more dangerous than is poverty without law.

Save a thief from the gallows and he will cut your throat.

Set a thief to catch a thief.

Sin that is hidden is half forgotten.

Sooner or later the truth comes to light.

Strict law is often great injustice.

Successful crime is called virtue.

Swindling is the perfection of civilisation.

That which is evil is soon learnt.

The back door robs the house.

The breastplate of innocence is not always scandal proof.

The devil finds work for idle hands to do.

The devil looks after his own.

The devil makes his Christmas pies of lawyers' tongues and clerks' fingers.

The devil take the hindmost.

The devil's children have the devil's luck.

The first of all virtues is innocence; modesty the
   second.

The gallows takes its own.

The good fear no law; it is his safety and the bad
   man's awe.

The good hate to sin from love of virtue, the bad hate
   to sin from fear of punishment.

The greater the sinner, the greater the saint.

The guilty mind needs no accuser.

The guilt and not the gallows makes the shame.

The judge is condemned when the accused is
   acquitted.

The law devised, it's evasion contrived.

The law guards us from all evils but itself.

The law has a nose of wax; one can twist it as he will.

The law is not the same at morning and night.

The laws sometimes sleep but never die.

The monarch's errors are forbidden game.

The more laws the less justice.

The more laws, the more offenders.

The most cunning are the first caught.

The prince and even the people are responsible for the crimes they neglect to punish.

The stains that villainy leave behind no time will wash away.

The sting of a reproach bears the truth of it.

The surest panoply is innocence.

The thief becomes the gallows well.

The thief is frightened even by the mouse.

The thief is sorry he is to be hanged, not that he is a thief.

The thief proceeds from a needle to gold, and from gold to the gallows.

The thief steals until he comes to the gallows.

The tongue always returns to the sore tooth.

The triumphing of the wicked is short.

The truth is the best advocate.

The villain's censure is extorted praise.

The wages of sin is death.

The wicked ears are deaf to wisdom's call.

The wickedness of a few is the calamity of all.

The wise man seeks the lawyer early.

The wolf calls the fox robber.

The wolf must pay with his skin.

The wolf prays not in his own field.

The worst punishment of all is that in the court of his own conscience, no guilty man is acquitted.

The wrong doer never lacks a pretext.

There are good and bad everywhere.

There are more thieves than are hanged.

There is but one short step between lying and theft.

There is honour among thieves.

There is no crime without a precedent.

They hurt themselves that do wrong.

They that dance must pay the fiddler.

Thieves quarrel and thefts are discovered.

Those whom guilt stains it equals.

Those who sow injustice reap hate and vengeance.

Though justice has leaden feet it has leaden hands.

Though malice may darken truth it cannot put it out.

'Tis not the action but the intention that is good or bad.

To a bad character good doctrine avails nothing.

To accuse the wicked and defend the wretched is an honour.

To err is human, to forgive divine.

To know the law and do the right are two different things.

Too much cunning undoes.

Trust makes way for treachery.

Truth and oil always come to the surface.

Truth is mighty and will prevail.

Truth is straight but judges are crooked.

Truth may be suppressed but never strangled.

Truth never fears investigation.

Truth never perishes.

Truth stretches but never breaks.

Truth's cloak is often lined with lies.

Two wrongs do not make a right.

Vice is its own punishment and sometimes its own
cure.

Vice is cherished and thrives by concealment.

Vice will stain the noblest race.

Virtue and vice cannot dwell under the same roof.

We are ever young enough to sin, never old enough to
repent.

We easily forget crimes known only to ourselves.

We ought to weigh well what we can only once
decide.

We should consult three things in all our actions;
justice, honesty and utility.

What can innocence hope for, when such as sit her judges are corrupted.

What is just and right is the law of laws.

What is no sin is no shame.

When God means to punish a nation He deprives its rulers of wisdom.

When it thunders the thief becomes honest.

When men of talents are punished, authority is strengthened.

When the cat is away the mice will play.

When thieves fall out, honest men come by their own.

Where law ends tyranny begins.

Where the wolf gets one lamb he looks for another.

Where vice is vengeance follows.

While you trust to the dog the wolf slips into the sheepfold.

Who demands justice must administer justice.

Who does no ill can have no foe.

Who does not punish evil invites it.

Who has deceived thee as often as thyself.

Who is not afraid of his sins, sins double.

Who punishes one threatens a hundred.

Who will not be deceived must have as many eyes on his head as hairs.

Woe be to him whose advocate becomes his accuser.

You are a fool to steal if you can't conceal.

You must not hang a man by his looks.

You'll dance at the end of a rope without teaching.

DEATH, SUFFERING AND GRIEF

A day of sorrow is longer than a month of joy.

A dead man does not make war.

A dead man does not speak.

A dead man has neither friends or relations.

A dead mouse feels no cold.

A drowning man will clutch at a straw.

A living dog is better than a dead lion.

A man can die but once.

A man has learned much, who has learned to die.

A small tear relieves a great sorrow.

A sudden death is the best.

All death is sudden to the unprepared.

All men are born richer than they die.

All sorrows are bearable if there is bread.

Alone in counsel, alone in sorrow.

An honourable death is worth more than an inglorious life.

Another's suffering is but skin deep.

Any mind that is capable of real sorrow is capable of real good.

As a man lives so shall he die.

As soon as man is born he begins to die.

As soon dies the calf as the cow.

As soon goes the lamb's skin to market as the old cow.

As the tree falls so shall it lie.

Bad news travels fast.

Better once dead than all the time suffering in need.

Better two losses than one sorrow.

Blessed are the dead that the rain falls on.

Blessed is the misfortune that comes alone.

Call no man happy till he dies.

Come soon or late death's undetermined day,
   This mortal being only can decay.

Constant complaints never get pity.

Curses, like chickens will come home to roost.

Dead dogs don't bite.

Dead folks can't bite.

Dead men do not bite.

Dead men pay no surgeons.

Dead men tell no tales.

Death always comes too early or too late.

Death and life are in the power of the tongue.

Death and love are two wings which bear men from
   earth to heaven.

Death defies the doctor.

Death does not blow a trumpet.

NATIONAL SUPERMARKETS
850 JUNGERMAN RD
03/08/95 12:16PM STORE   22
CUST 121 REG 2 OPR   135

  .55LB @ .49/ LB
GREEN BEANS   .27*T
INT L DLITE AMAR   .99*T
INT L DLITE AMAR   .99*T
INT L DLITE AMAR   .99*T
SPLIT PEAS   .25*T
     TOTAL $ 3.74
     CASH TEND   5.00

     SUBTOTAL   3.49
     TAX PAID   .25

  1.26 CHANGE

   COUPON SUMMARY
  5   ITEMS   3.49

   YOU'RE IMPORTANT TO

Death foreseen never comes.

Death has a thousand doors to let out life.

Death hath nothing terrible in it, but what life hath
    made so.

Death is a black camel that kneels at every man's
    gate.

Death is but what the haughty brave,
    The weak must bear, the wretch must crave.

Death is in the pot.

Death is never premature except to those who die
    without virtue.

Death is not the greatest of ills; it is worse to want to
    die, and not be able to.

Death is shameful in flight, glorious in victory.

Death is the great leveller.

Death keeps no calendar.

Death meets us everywhere.

Death opens the gate to good fame and extinguishes
    envy.

Death pays all debts.

Death rather frees us of ills than robs us of our goods.

Death is but a path that must be trod,
  If man would ever pass to God.

Death spares neither pope nor beggar.

Death spares neither man nor beast.

Death to the wolf is life to the lamb.

Death will hear of no excuse.

Deep swimmers and high climbers seldom die in their beds.

Desperate diseases must have desperate remedies.

Dig but deep enough, and under all earth runs water, under all life runs grief.

Do not speak ill of the dead, but deem them sacred who have gone into the immortal state.

Earth has no sorrow that heaven cannot heal.

Every cloud has a silver lining.

Every man must eat a peck of dust before he dies.

Every one can master a grief but he that has it.

Every one must pay his debt to nature.

Every substantial grief has twenty shadows, and most of them shadows of your own making.

Everything becomes intolerable to the man who is once subdued by grief.

Few have luck, all have death.

Good or bad we must all live.

Great griefs are mute.

Great griefs medicine the less.

Great pains cease us to forget the little ones.

Grey hairs are death's blossoms.

Grief diminishes when it has nothing to grow upon.

Grief is a stone that bears one down, but two bear it lightly.

Grief is satisfied and carried off by tears.

Grief is the agony of an instant; the indulgence of grief the blunder of a life.

Grief pent up will break the heart.

Hang sorrow, care will kill the cat.

He dies like a beast who has done no good while he lived.

He gains enough who loses sorrow.

He grieves more than is necessary who grieves before it is necessary.

He hath not lived that lives not after death.

He hauls at a long rope that expects another's death.

He is miserable indeed who must lock up his miseries.

He is miserable once who feels it, but twice who fears it before it comes.

He lives in fame who dies for virtue's cause

He should wear iron shoes that bides his neighbour's death.

He that conceals his grief finds no remedy for it.

He that died half a year ago is as dead as Adam.

He that dies this year is quit of the next.

He that is uneasy at ever so little pain is never without some ache.

DEATH, SUFFERING AND GRIEF

He that lives long suffers much.

He that lives most, dies most.

He that lives not well for one year sorrows it for
seven.

He that lives on hope has but a slender diet.

He waits long that waits for another man's death.

He who cannot hold his peace will never live at ease.

He who fears death dies every time he thinks of it.

He who lives on hope dies on hunger.

He who loves sorrow will always find something to
grieve over.

He who much has suffered much will know.

He who swims in sin will sink in sorrow.

Help you to salt, help you to sorrow.

Hope deferred makes a sick heart.

Hope for the best and prepare for the worst.

How wise in God to place death at the end of life.

If death be terrible the fault is not in death but thee.

If you want to be dead wash your head and go to bed.

Immoderate sorrow causes great mischief.

It is a great art to laugh at your own misfortunes.

It is a great journey to life's end.

It is as natural to die as to be born.

It is better to die once than to live always in the fear of death.

It is good to die before one has done anything deserving death.

It is good to see in the misfortunes of others what we should avoid.

It is hard even for the most miserable to die.

It is not work that kills but worry.

It is poor comfort for one who has broken his leg that another has broken his neck.

It is the lot of man to suffer.

It never rains but it pours.

Its ill waiting for dead men's shoes.

Keep thine eye fixed on the end of life.

Let pain deserved without complaint be borne.

Let the dead bury the dead.

Let us eat and drink for tomorrow we shall die.

Life ain't all beer and skittles.

Life and misery began together.

Life goes on.

Life is a road beset with roses and thorns.

Life is a state of warfare.

Life is labour, death is rest.

Life is not to be bought with heaps of gold.

Life would be too smooth if it had no rubs in it.

Light sorrows speak, great ones are dumb.

Make not two sorrows of one.

Many a one suffers for what he cannot help.

Men fear death as children go in the dark.

Misery acquaints a man with strange bedfellows.

Misery doth brave minds abate.

Misery is always unjust.

Misery loves company.

Misfortune does not always come to injure.

Misfortune is a good teacher.

Misfortunes never come singly.

Much of grief shows still some want of wit.

Never say die.

Never speak ill of the dead.

New grief awakens the old.

No day passes without some grief.

No man can be ignorant that he must die, nor be sure
   that he may not this very day.

No news is good news.

No priority among the dead.

No young man believes he shall ever die.

Nothing dries sooner than a tear.

Nothing is certain in this world but death and taxes.

Nothing is so bad that it might have been worse.

Of the great and of the dead, either speak well or say nothing.

Of thy sorrow be not too sad, of thy joy be not too glad.

Old men go to death, death comes to young men.

Old soldiers never die.

One funeral makes many.

Our griefs how swift, our remedies how slow.

Our own grief produces pity for another.

Pain makes even the innocent liars.

Pale death knocks at the cottage and the palace with an impartial hand.

Rejoice not in another's sorrow.

Sacred even to gods, is misery.

She grieves sincerely who grieves unseen.

Shrouds have no pockets.

Sin and sorrow are inseparable.

Six feet of earth makes all men equal.

So live and hope as if thou would die immediately.

So long as the sick man has life there is hope.

Sorrow concealed doth burn the heart to cinders.

Sorrow dwells on the confines of pleasure.

Sorrows remembered sweeten present joy.

Stone dead hat no fellow.

Suffer in order to know, toil in order to have.

Sufferings are lessons.

Tears are sometimes as weighty as words.

Tears benefit not the dead, they may injure the living.

Tears in mortal miseries are vain.

The actions of a dying man are void of disguise.

The best cure for sorrow is to pity somebody.

The bitter pill may have wholesome effects.

The bitterness of death must be tasted by him who is
   to appreciate the sweetness of deliverance.

The bridge between joy and sorrow is not long.

The darkest hour is just before the dawn.

The dead and absent have no friends.

The dead are soon forgotten.

The dead govern the living.

The dead man is unenvied.

The dead open the eyes of the living.

The evening praises the day, death the life.

The fewer his years the fewer his tears.

The first breath is the beginning of death.

The good die young.

The greatest business of life is to prepare for death.

The grief of the heir is only masked laughter.

The holidays of joy are the vigils of sorrow.

The miseries of the virtuous are the scandal of the
   good.

The only cure for grief is action.

The road of death must be travelled by us all.

The sharper the storm, the sooner its over.

The sorrow men have for others hangs upon a hair.

The sublimest grief will eat at last.

The sun and death are two things we cannot stare in the face.

The tears of the night equal the smiles of the day.

There is a remedy for everything except death.

There is no greater misfortune than not to be able to bear misfortune.

There is no pain so great that time will not soften.

There is no remembrance which time does not obliterate, nor pain which death does not put an end to.

They that live longest must die at last.

They truly mourn that mourn without a witness.

Those who have known grief seldom seem sad.

They who live in a worry invite death in a hurry.

Three may keep a secret if two of them are dead.

Time and thinking tame the strongest grief.

Time goes, death comes.

Time is a great healer.

To grief there is a limit, not so to fear.

To live in the hearts we leave behind us is not to die.

Too late to grieve when the chance is past.

Two in distress make sorrow less.

Until death there is no knowing what may befall.

We die as we live.

We must live by the quick, not by the dead.

We must suffer much or die young.

We shall lie all alike in our graves.

When misery is highest, help is nearest.

When one is dead it is for a long time.

When sorrow is asleep wake it not.

When you die even your tomb shall be comfortable.

When you die your trumpeter will be buried.

Where a man feels pain he lays his hand.

Wherever we meet misery we owe pity.

While there is life there is hope.

Who dies in youth and vigour dies best.

Who has no plagues makes himself some.

Who often changes, suffers.

Who thinks often of death does nothing worthy of life.

Whom the Gods love die young.

You can only die once.

You cannot shift an old tree without it dying.

ENTERPRISE AND COMMERCE

A carpenter is known by his chips.

A good beginning is half the work.

A good head and industrious hand are worth gold in any land.

A handful of trade is a handful of gold.

A journey of a thousand miles begins with a single step.

A man can do no more than he can.

A man of words and not of deeds is like a garden full of weeds.

A man without a smiling face must not open a shop.

A ploughman on his legs is higher than a gentleman on his knees.

A poor workman blames his tools.

A weak foundation destroys the work.

A work ill done must be done twice.

A work well begun is half done.

Absence of occupation is not rest.

Adversity makes men, prosperity monsters.

Adversity overcome is the highest glory.

All work and no play makes Jack a dull boy.

Ambition has no rest.

Ambition is no cure for love.

An oak is not felled at one stroke.

Attempt not or accomplish.

Attempt nothing beyond your strength.

Be not a baker if your head be of butter.

Begin in time to finish without hurry.

Better direct well than work hard.

Better sit idle than work for nothing.

Blind ambition quite mistakes her road.

Boldness in business is the fist, second, and third thing.

Business before pleasure.

Business is the salt of life.

Business makes a man as well as tries him.

Business neglected is business lost.

Business sweetens pleasure, and labour sweetens rest.

Buy in the cheapest market and sell in the dearest.

By the hands of many a great work is made light.

By the work we know the workman.

By work you get money, by talk you get knowledge.

Cheap things are not good, good things are not cheap.

Climb not too high lest the fall be the greater.

Commerce loves freedom.

Creditors have better memories than debtors.

Defer not till tomorrow what may be done today.

Diligent work makes a skilful workman.

Do business, be not a slave to it.

Do not neglect your own field and plough your neighbours.

Do the head work before the hand work.

Don't have too many irons in the fire or some will be sure to burn.

Drive thy business, let not that drive thee.

Early to bed and early to rise, makes a man healthy, wealthy and wise.

Every man as his business lies.

Every man does his own business best.

Every man is the architect of his own fortune.

Every trade has its ways.

Everybody's business is nobody's business.

Faith will move mountains.

First come, first served.

Follow the river and you will find the sea.

Fortune favours the brave.

Fortune knocks at least once on every man's door.

From small beginnings come great things.

Fuel is not sold in a forest, nor fish on a lake.

God helps them that help themselves.

Good material is half the work.

Good works will never save you but you cannot be saved without them.

Great gain makes work easy.

He is a poor workman who cannot talk of work.

He that comes first to the hill may sit where he will.

He that heweth above his height may have a chip in his eye.

He that is ashamed of his calling ever lives shamefully in it.

He that labours is tempted by one devil and he that is idle by a thousand.

He that thinks his business below him will always be above his business.

He never wrought a good day's work that went about grumbling about it.

He who does not advance recedes.

He who hesitates is lost.

He who toils with pain will eat with pleasure.

He who wills the end, wills the means.

If a thing is worth doing it is worth doing well.

If at first you don't succeed; try, try again.

If you don't make mistakes you'll never make anything.

If you want a thing done properly, do it yourself.

In all labour there is profit.

In for a penny, in for a pound.

Industry is fortune's right hand, and frugality her left.

Industry pays debts but despair increases them.

It is better to travel hopefully than to arrive.

It is easier said than done.

It is for want of application rather than of means that men fail of success.

It is lost labour to sow where there is no soil.

It is more noble to make yourself great than to be born so.

It is the first step that is difficult.

It's all in the day's work.

Jack of all trades and master of none.

Keep thy shop and thy shop will keep thee.

Labour has a bitter root but a sweet taste.

Life gives nothing to man without great labour.

Make hay while the sun shines.

Man works from sun to sun, a woman's work is never done.

Many a man labours for the day he may never live to see.

Many hands make light work.

Mighty work must be done with few words.

Mind no business but your own.

Necessity is the mother of invention.

Necessity never made a good bargain.

Never cross a bridge until you come to it.

Never pay your workman beforehand.

Never send a boy to do a man's job.

No gain without pain.

Not to oversee workmen is to leave your purse open.

Nothing is achieved without toil.

Nothing succeeds like success

Nothing ventured, nothing gained.

One door never shuts but another opens.

Pity and compassion spoil business.

Punctuality is the soul of business.

Put a stout heart to a steep hill.

Reward sweetens labour.

Rome was not built in a day.

Seek and ye shall find.

Slow work produces fine goods.

Sour work, sweet sleep.

Strike while the iron is hot.

Success has many fathers while failure is an orphan.

Tall oaks from little acorns grow.

The buyer has need of a hundred eyes, the seller but of one.

The customer is always right.

The difficult is done at once, the impossible takes a little longer.

The end must justify the means.

The higher the monkey climbs the more he shows his tail.

The labourer is worthy of his hire.

The longest road is the shortest way home.

The result tests the work.

The time is never lost that is devoted to work.

The work praises the workman.

There are many rare abilities in the world that fortune never brings to light.

There is always room at the top.

There is no eel so small it does not expect to become a whale.

There is no such thing as a free lunch.

They conquer who believe they can.

Think of ease, but work on.

Thy hand is never the worse for doing thy own work.

To make a man of yourself you must toil.

To the brave and faithful nothing is difficult.

Toil is prayer.

Too many cooks spoil the broth.

What is a workman without tools.

Whatever has been attained is attainable.

When toil ceases the people suffer.

Where bees are, there is honey.

Where there is a will there is a way.

Where there is muck there is money.

Who begins too much accomplishes little.

Who hath a good trade through all waters may wade.

Work first and then rest.

Work makes the workman.

Work produces virtue, and virtue honour.

Workmen are easier found than masters.

You can't win them all.

You cannot get blood from a stone.

You cannot make bricks without straw.

You must speculate to accumulate.

You never know what you can do until you try.

FAMILY AND FRIENDS

A babe in the house is a well spring of pleasure.

A babe is a mother's anchor, she cannot swing far from her moorings.

A babe is an angel whose wings decrease as his legs increase.

A broken friendship may be soldered but will never be sound.

A brother's sufferings claim a brother's pity.

A bustling mother makes a slothful daughter.

A child may have too much of his mother's blessing.

A child's back must be bent early.

A clear bargain, a dear friend.

A courageous is better than a cowardly friend.

A fair weather friend changes with the wind.

A faithful friend is the true image of the deity.

A false friend and a shadow attend only when the sun shines.

A false friend has honey in his mouth, gall in his heart.

A false friend is worse than an open enemy.

A father is a treasure, a brother a comfort, but a friend is both.

A father lives after the death of his son.

A father loves his children in hating their faults.

A father maintains ten children better than ten children one father.

A father's blessing cannot be drowned in water nor consumed by fire.

A father's love for all others is air.

A favourite has no friends.

A foe to God was never true friend to man.

A fond mother produces mischief.

A friend and look to thyself.

A friend as far as conscience allows.

A friend at one's back is a safe bridge.

A friend cannot be known at the market.

A friend cannot be known in prosperity nor an enemy hidden in adversity.

A friend in need is a friend in deed.

A friend in the market is better than money in the chest.

A friend is best found in adversity.

A friend is never known until needed.

A friend is not known till he is lost.

A friend is not so soon found as lost.

A friend is to be taken with his faults.

A friend loves at all times, and a brother is born for adversity.

A friend; one soul, two bodies.

A friend should bear a friend's infirmities.

A friend that you buy with presents will be bought from you.

A friend to everybody is a friend to nobody.

A friend without faults will never be found.

A friend's dinner is soon dressed.

A friend's faults should be known but not abhorred.

A friend's frown is better than a fool's smile.

A good-natured friend is often only an enemy in disguise.

A good friend is better than silver or gold.

A good friend is my nearest relation.

A good friend never offends.

A good master of the house must be first to bed and first out.

A good mother does not hear the music of the dance when her children cry.

A hedge between keeps friendships green.

A lame mule and a stupid son have to endure everything.

A landmark is well placed between two brothers fields.

A little absence does much good.

A lost friendship is an enmity won.

A man, a dog, and a horse never tire of each other's company.

A man is known by the company he keeps.

A man may see his friend need but will not see him bleed.

A man without a friend is only half a man.

A man would not be alone even in paradise.

A mother is a mother all the days of her life, a father is a father 'til he gets a new wife.

A mother's heart is always with her children.

A mother's love changes never.

A mother's love is best of all.

A near neighbour is better than a distant cousin.

A ready way to lose a friend is to lend him money.

A reconciled friend is half an enemy.

A rich friend is a treasure.

A small family is soon provided for.

A son pays his father's debts, but a father will not recognise his son's.

A son-in-law's friendship is a winter's sun.

A sure friend is known in a doubtful case.

A table friend is changeable.

A thousand friend are few, one foe many.

A trouble shared is a trouble halved.

A true friend does sometimes venture to be offensive.

A true friend is above all things capital.

A true friend is forever a friend.

A wise son makes a glad father, but a foolish son is the heaviness of his mother.

Absence doth but hold off a friend to make one see him more clearly.

Absent or dead still let a friend be dear.

Admonish your friends in private, praise them in public.

All are not friends who speak one fair.

An Englishman's home is his castle.

An ill father desires not an ill son.

An old friend is better than two new ones.

An old mother in the house is a hedge.

An unpeaceable man hath no neighbour.

An untried friend is like an uncracked nut.

As the field, so the crops; as the father so the sons.

As the mother so the daughter.

At first babes feed on the mother's bosom, but always on her heart.

At weddings and funerals friends are discovered from kinsfolk.

Avoid a friend who covers you with his wings and destroys you with his beak.

Be a friend to thyself and others will be so too.

Be blind to the failings of your friends but never to their vices.

Before you make a friend eat a peck of salt with him.

Behold thy friend and of thyself the pattern see.

Better a good cow than a cow of good kind.

Better foes than hollow friends.

Better have a friend in the marketplace than money in your coffer.

Better have a friend on the road than gold or silver in your purse.

Better lose a jest than a friend.

Better is a neighbour that is near than a brother that is far off.

Better the child cry than the mother sigh.

Between two brothers two witnesses and a notary.

Birds of a feather flock together.

Blood is thicker than water.

Blood will tell.

Bought friends are not friends in deed.

By requiting one friend we invite many.

Ceremony is the cloak of friendship.

Charity begins at home.

Chasten thy son while there is hope.

Children are certain cares.

Children sweeten labours, but they make misfortunes more bitter.

Children tell in the highway what they hear by the fireside.

Children when little make parents fools, when great mad.

Come live with me and you shall know me.

Daughters are easy to rear but difficult to marry.

Daughters can never take too much care of their fathers.

Disparity of fortune is the bane of friendship.

Even as the father was so shall the son be.

Even reckoning keeps long friends.

Every mother's child is handsome.

Every one can keep house better than her mother till she tries.

Everything goes by favour and cousinship.

Faithful are the wounds of a friend.

Fall sick and you will find who your friend is and who is not.

Familiarity breeds contempt.

Fate chooses our relatives, we choose our friends.

Fathers in reclaiming a child should outwit him and seldom beat him.

Fish and guests stink after three days.

Forget not the mother that fondled you at the breast.

Fresh fish and poor friends soon grow ill favoured.

Friends agree best at a distance.

Friends and mules fail us at hard passes.

Friends are born not made.

Friends are far from the man who is unfortunate.

Friends are like fiddle strings, they must not be screwed too tight.

Friends are thieves of time.

Friends got without desert are lost without cause.

Friends may meet, but mountains never greet.

Friends need no formal invitation.

Friends tie their purses with cobweb strings.

Friendship always benefits; love sometimes injures.

Friendship is a sheltering tree.

Friendship is love with understanding.

Friendship is not bought at the fair.

Friendship is the perfection of love.

Friendship is the wine of life.

Friendship should be unpicked not rent.

Friendships multiply joys and divide griefs.

From clogs to clogs is only three generations.

From shirtsleeves to shirtsleeves in three generations.

From the father comes honour, from the mother, comfort.

Give me a child for the first seven years and you may do what you like with him afterwards.

Give to a pig when it grunts and to a child when it cries, and you will have a fine pig and a bad child.

Go slowly to the entertainments of thy friends and quickly to their misfortunes.

God could not be everywhere, therefore he made mothers.

God keep me from my friends, from my enemies I will keep myself.

Good company makes short miles.

Greatness of name in the father oft-times overwhelms the son.

Happy is he that is happy in his children.

Happy is he whose friends were born before him.

He does not sing his father's song.

He has made a younger brother of him.

He is a good friend who speaks well of us behind our backs.

He is my friend that grinds at my mill.

He is no friend that eats his own by himself, and mine with me.

He makes no friend who never made a foe.

He never was a friend who ceased to be so.

He that bring up his son to nothing breeds a thief.

He that has no fools, knaves or beggars in his family was begot by a flash of lightning.

He that is absent will not be the heir.

He that obliges me in a strange country makes himself my brother.

He that seeks to have many friends never has any.

He that would have many friends should try a few of them.

He to whom God gave no sons the devil gives nephews.

He who cannot counterfeit a friend, can never be a dangerous enemy.

He who for his own sake would expose a friend deserves not to have any.

He who has a good nest finds good friends.

He who has a thousand friends has not a friend to
   spare, he who has one enemy shall meet him
   everywhere.

He who has daughters to marry let him give them silk
   to spin.

He who picks up the staff of his father with respect
   will not beat his dog.

He who takes the child by the hand takes the mother
   by the heart.

His mother an onion, his father garlic, himself comes
   out a conserve of roses.

Home is home, though it's never so homely.

Home is where the heart is.

If you want enemies excel others, if you want friends
   let others excel you.

In time of prosperity friends will be plenty,
   In time of adversity not one among twenty.

Instinctive, unlike rational affection, has no favourite.

It costs something to support a family, however small.

It is a good friend that is always giving though it be
   never so little.

It is a wise child that knows its own father.

It is better to be the best of a low family than the worst of a noble one.

It is good to have friends everywhere.

It is good to have friends in high places.

It is more disgraceful to suspect our friends than to be deceived by them.

It is not the anger of the father but his silence that the well-born son dreads.

It takes three generations to make a gentleman.

Keep your own fish-guts for your own sea-maws.

Leave your son a good reputation and employment.

Lend your money and lose your friend.

Life without a friend is death without a witness.

Like breeds like.

Like father like son.

Like mother like daughter.

Like will to like.

Long absence changes friends.

Long absent soon forgotten.

May God not prosper our friends that they forget us.

Mother's love is ever in its spring.

Mother's truth keeps constant youth.

My friend is he that helps me in time of need.

My friend's enemy is often my best friend.

My son is my son till he gets him a wife, but my
  daughter's my daughter all the days of her life

No advice like a fathers.

No ape but swears he has the handsomest children.

No better friend than the man himself.

No mother is so wicked but she desires to have good
  children.

None of us like the crying of another one's baby.

Nothing can be sweeter than friendship.

Nothing so dangerous as an ignorant friend.

Of brothers-in-law and red dogs few are good.

Old friends and new reckoning.

Old friends and old wine are best.

Old tunes are sweetest and old friends are surest.

Once a buffoon, never the good father of a family.

One good turn deserves another.

One seldom finds white ravens and true friends.

One tear of a mother can blot out a thousand
complaints against her.

Our domestic affections are the most salutary basis of
all good government.

Own brothers keep careful accounts.

Patched up friendship seldom becomes whole again.

Praise the child and make love to the mother.

Save us from our friends.

She spins a good web that brings up her son well.

So yourself be good, a fig for your grandfather.

Spare the rod and spoil the child.

Sudden friendship, sure repentance.

Suffering for a friend doubles friendship.

The apple never falls far from the tree.

The best of friends must part.

The brother had rather see the sister rich than make her so.

The child is father to the man.

The company makes the feast.

The family that prays together, stays together.

The father a saint, the son a devil.

The father in praising his son extols himself.

The father sighs more at the death of one son than at the birth of many.

The father to the bough, the son to the plough.

The father's virtue is the child's best inheritance.

The fire burns brightest on one's own hearth.

The friendship of the great is fraternity with lions.

The greatest blessing is a true friend.

The hand that rocks the cradle rules the world.

The husband's mother is the wife's devil.

The joys of parents are secret, and so are their griefs and fears.

The more acquaintances the more danger.

The mother knows best whether the child be like the father.

The mother of a coward does not often weep.

The mother of a timid son never weeps.

The mother reckons well, but the child reckons better.

The mother's breath is always sweet.

The mother-in-law must be entreated and the pot must be let stand.

The only reward of virtue is virtue; the only way to have a friend is to be one.

The ornament of the house is the friends who frequent it.

The portrait of the father is but a picture to the stranger, to the son a book which points out his duties.

The shoemaker's son will always go barefoot.

The son disgraces himself when he blames the father.

The son that yawns at his father's oft repeated stories will weep little at his death.

The tardy son reaps not with his father.

The ungrateful son is a wart on his father's face; to leave it is a blemish, to cut it off is a pain.

The vulgar estimate friends by the advantage to be derived from them.

The wrath of brothers is the wrath of devils.

The younger brother hath the more wit.

The younger brother is the ancient gentleman.

There can be no friendship where there is no freedom.

True friendship is imperishable.

Upon my family at home depends my character abroad.

Walnuts and pears you plant for your heirs.

We carry our neighbour's failings in sight; we throw our own over our shoulders.

We think our fathers fools, so wise we grow,
Our wiser sons will think us so.

Wife and children are bills of charges.

What is sucked in with the mother's milk runs out in the shroud.

When a friend asks there is no tomorrow.

When good cheer is lacking, our friends will be packing.

When the blind lead the blind they both shall fall in the ditch.

When there are two friends to one purse, the one sings, the other weeps.

When two fall out the third wins.

Where can one be happier than in the bosom of his family.

Where there are friends there are riches.

Who chatters to you will chatter of you.

Who has gold can choose his son-in-law.

Who has no son has no satisfaction.

Who makes friends of all keeps none.

Whom we love best, to them we can say least.

Whom will he help that does not help his mother.

Without a friend the world is a wilderness.

Without hearts it is no home.

Write down the advice of him that loves you though you like it not at present.

You may thank God your father was born before you.

You scratch my back and I'll scratch yours.

You should know a man seven years before you stir his fire.

FOOD AND DRINK

A black plum is as sweet as a white.

A day without bread is a long day indeed.

A drunkard's purse is a bottle.

A drunken man may soon be made to dance.

A full stomach studies unwillingly.

A good eater must be a good man.

A man hath often more trouble to get food than to digest it.

A man that has had his fill is no eater.

A meal without wine is like a day without sunshine.

A rotten egg cannot be spoiled.

FOOD AND DRINK

A sharp stomach makes a short devotion.

After dinner rest awhile, after supper walk awhile

After sweet meat comes sour sauce.

Ale sellers should not be tale tellers.

All is fish that comes to the net.

All is grist that comes to the mill.

All meat is not the same in every man's mouth.

Always rise from the table with an appetite and you
will never sit down without one.

An army marches on its stomach.

An old dram drinker is the devil's decoy.

As a man eats so he works.

As you bake so shall ye brew.

Better a dinner of herbs than a stalled ox where hate
is.

Better half an egg than an empty shell.

Better weak beer than an empty cask.

Bread is the staff of life.

Bread of a day, ale of a month, and wine of a year.

Butter spoils no meat and moderation no cause.

Cheese and bread make the cheek red.

Cheese is gold in the morning, silver at noon and lead at night.

Drink and drouth come not always together.

Drink little that ye may drink long.

Drink in the morning staring, and in the evening sparing.

Drink nothing without seeing it, sign nothing without reading it.

Drink upon salad costs doctor a ducat, drink upon eggs costs him two.

Drink washes off the daub and discovers the man.

Drink wine and have the gout, drink nothing and have it too.

Drink wine and let the water go to the mill.

Drinking kindness is drunken friendship.

Drunkenness does not produce faults; it uncovers them.

Drunkenness is a bewitching devil, a pleasant poison and a sweet sin.

Drunkenness is a pair of spectacles to see the devil and all his works.

Drunkenness is an egg from which all vices are hatched.

Drunkenness is nothing but voluntary madness.

Drunkenness turns a man out of himself and leaves a beast in his room.

Drunkenness makes some men fools, some beasts and some devils.

Drunken folk seldom take harm.

Eat a bit before you drink.

Eat at pleasure, drink by measure.

Eat bread that is light and cheese by weight.

Eat peas with the king and cherries with the beggar.

Eaten bread is soon forgotten.

Eating and drinking make the stomach full but the purse empty.

Every animal but man keeps to one dish.

Every cook praises his own broth.

Fiddlers, dogs and fleas come to a feast uncalled.

First catch your hare and then cook it.

Fresh pork and new wine, kill a man before his time.

God sends meat, but the devil sends cooks.

Good ale is meat, drink and cloth.

Good drink drives out bad thoughts.

Good wine is milk for the aged.

Good wine makes a bad head and a long story.

Good wine makes good blood.

Good wine praises itself.

Good wine ruins the purse and bad the stomach.

He that banquets every day never makes a good meal.

He that eats and saves sets his table twice.

He that eats most porridge shall have most meat.

He thinks of everything who wants of bread.

He who has drunk will drink.

He who likes drinking is always talking of wine.

Hunger is the best sauce.

Hungry men think the cook lazy.

In the looking-glass we see the form, in wine the heart.

Inflaming wine dulls the noble heart.

It is an ill cook that cannot lick his own fingers.

It is the stomach that bears the feet.

Let the drunkard alone and he will fall of himself.

Man cannot live by bread alone.

Man is what he eats.

Many a good drop of broth is made in an old pot.

Of what use is the golden cup if the wine in it be sour

Of wine the middle, of oil the top and of honey the bottom is best.

Often drunk and seldom sober falls like the leaves in October.

Old wood to burn, old wine to drink.

One does not eat acorns when he has peaches.

Only what I drink is mine.

Passion makes a man a beast, but wine makes him worse.

Salt spilt is never all gathered.

Send not for a hatchet with which to break open the egg.

Since the wine is drawn it must be drunk.

Small choice in rotten apples.

Small stomachs, light heels.

Sour grapes can never make sweet wine.

Spilt wine is worse than water.

Starve together, eat together.

Stolen bread stirs the appetite.

Stranger's meat is the greatest treat.

Sweet is the apple when the keeper is away.

Sweet wine makes sour vinegar.

Sweets to the sweet.

The appetite comes with the eating.

The best cure for drunkenness is while sober to see a drunken man.

The counsels that are given in wine, Will do no good to thee or thine.

The drunkard is discovered by his praise of wine.

The drunken man's joy is often the sober man's sorrow.

The drunken mouth reveals the heart's secrets.

The eggs do not teach the hen.

The first draught a man drinks ought to be for thirst, the second for nourishment, the third for pleasure, and the fourth for madness.

The nearer the bone the sweeter the meat.

The proof of the pudding is in the eating.

The smaller the drink the cooler the blood and the clearer the head.

The stew that boils much loses its flavour.

The stomach is a shopkeeper that gives no credit.

The stomach is easier filled than the eye.

The stomach rules the head.

The way to a man's heart is through his stomach.

The well fed man does not believe in hunger.

The wise drunkard is a sober fool.

There are more old drunkards than old doctors.

There is no such witness as a good measure of wine.

There is no sweet without sour.

They that drink longest live longest.

Thick wine is better than clear water.

Thirst makes wine out of water.

Thoughts when sober, said when drunk.

Thousands drink themselves to death before one dies of thirst.

To good eating belongs good drinking.

To the hungry no bread is bad.

Too many cooks spoil the broth.

Truth and folly dwell in the wine cask.

Water is the best of all things.

Water is the strongest drink; it drives mills.

What is in the heart of the sober man is on the tongue of the drunken man.

What is sauce for the goose is sauce for the gander.

What soberness conceals drunkenness reveals.

What the sober man thinks the drunkard tells.

What you do when drunk you must pay for when sober.

What's sauce for the goose is sauce for the gander.

When the stomach is full the heart is glad.

Where the best wine is grown the worst is drank.

Where there is milk in the can for one there is milk in the can for two.

While the pot boils friendship blooms.

Who eats and leaves has another good meal.

Who eats his dinner alone must saddle his horse alone.

Wine in the bottle will not quench the thirst.

Wine will not keep in a foul vessel.

You can't have your cake and eat it.

You can't make an omelette without breaking eggs.

You must take the fat with the lean.

You never miss your water until your well runs dry.

You spoil a good dish with ill sauce.

FOOLS AND FOLLY

A barber learns to shave by shaving fools.

A braying ass eats little hay.

A cucumber being offered a poor man he refused it because it was crooked.

A fair promise makes a fool merry.

A flatterer is the shadow of a fool.

A fool always comes short of his reckoning.

A fool always finds a greater fool than himself.

A fool always finds a greater fool to admire him.

A fool and his money are soon parted.

A fool at forty is a fool indeed.

DICTIONARY OF PROVERBS

A fool bolts a door with a boiled carrot.

A fool brings a staff to beat his own head.

A fool can dance without a fiddle.

A fool cannot be silent.

A fool cut down the oak to plant a thistle.

A fool demands much, but he is a greater that gives it.

A fool digs a well by the river.

A fool expects that larks will fall ready roasted into his own mouth.

A fool expects to find water at the first stroke of his spade.

A fool fights with his own shadow.

A fool fishes in the air and hunts in the sea.

A fool fouls the stream and expects it to be pure.

A fool has given a hen for an egg.

A fool if he holds his tongue passes for wise.

A fool is always meditating how he can begin his life, a wise man how he can end it.

124

A fool is better than an obstinate man.

A fool is one who gives, a greater one who will not take.

A fool is the wise man's ladder.

A fool killed the goose that laid the golden egg.

A fool laughs when others laugh.

A fool may chance to say a wise thing.

A fool may make money but it takes a wise man to spend it.

A fool must now and then be right by chance.

A fool never admires himself so much as when he has committed a folly.

A fool only wins the first game.

A fool pulled down the house for the sake of the mortar.

A fool put the cart before the horse.

A fool put water into a basket.

A fool sees not the same tree that a wise man sees.

A fool thinks nothing right but what he does himself.

A fool wants his cloak on a rainy day.

A fool when he hath spoken hath done all.

A fool who speaks the truth is better than a hundred liars.

A fool will be foiled.

A fool will laugh when he is drowning.

A fool's bolt is soon shot.

A fool's heart dances on his lips.

A fool's tongue is long enough to cut his own throat.

A lazy boy and a warm bed are hard to part.

A madman and a fool are no witnesses.

A man is a stark fool all the time he is angry.

A man never appreciates ashes until he slips on the ice.

A man's folly is his worst foe and his discretion his best friend.

A man's folly ought to be his greatest secret.

A nod for a wise man and a rod for a fool.

A pointless saying is a fool's doing.

A rolling stone gathers no moss.

A vacant mind is open to all suggestions, as a hollow mountain returns all sounds.

A wager is a fool's argument.

A wise man associating with the vicious becomes an idiot, a dog travelling with good men becomes a rational being.

A wise man begins in the end and a fool ends in the beginning.

A wise man may look ridiculous in the company of fools.

A wise man thinks all that he says, a fool says all that he thinks.

A wise man will not reprove a fool.

A wise man's thoughts walk within him, a fool's without him.

Advice to a fool goes in one ear and out the other.

All asses do not go on four feet.

All but fools know fear sometimes.

All fails that fools think.

All the fools are not dead yet.

An ass does not hit himself twice against the same stone.

An ass is but an ass though laden with gold.

An ass let him be who brays at an ass.

An ass will deny more in an hour than a hundred philosophers will prove in a hundred years.

An easy fool is a knave's tool.

Anger begins with folly and ends in repentance.

Anger may glance into the breast of a wise man, but rests only in the bosom of fools.

Ashes always fly back in the face of him that throws them.

Ask a silly question and get a silly answer.

Avarice is both knave and fool.

Better a witty fool than a foolish wit.

Better to weep with the wise man than to laugh with the fool.

Better with the wise in prison than the fools in
  paradise.

Between two stools one falls to the ground.

Big head, little wit.

Buffoonery and scurrility are the corruption of wit, as
  knavery is of wisdom.

Careless shepherds make many a feast for the wolf.

Children and fools are prophets.

Children and fools have merry lives.

Children and fools should not see half done work.

Children and fools tell the truth.

Do not ask which is the right way from a blind man.

Do not bite the hand that feeds you.

Drunkards have a fool's tongue and a knave's heart.

Each wise man has a fool for his brother.

Empty vessels make the most sound.

Even a fool can bet a good hand at poker.

Even an ass will not fall twice in the same quicksand.

Every ass thinks himself worthy to stand with the king's horses.

Every fool is pleased with his bauble.

Every fool will be meddling.

Every potter praises his own pot and the more if it be cracked.

Experience keeps a dear school; but fools will learn in no other.

Experience is the mistress of fools.

Flattery is the food of fools.

Folly and learning oft dwell together.

Folly as well as wisdom is justified by it's children.

Fool's names, like fool's faces are often seen in public places.

Fools and madmen ought not to be left in their own company.

Fools are free the whole world over.

Fools are known by looking wise.

Fools ask questions that wise men cannot answer.

Fools build houses and wise men live in them.

Fools for luck.

Fools invent fashions and wise men follow them.

Fools rush in where angels fear to tread.

Fools set stools for wise men to stumble at.

For want of a horseshoe nail a kingdom was lost.

Forbid a fool a thing and that he'll do.

Fortune favours fools.

From the fool and the drunkard you may learn the
truth.

Halfwitted folk speak much and say little.

He calls for the shoeing horn to help on his gloves.

He catches the wind with a net.

He chastises the dead.

He draws water with a sieve.

He gives grass to the lion and meat to the horse.

He gives straw to his dog and bones to his ass.

He hath some wit but a great fool hath the guidance of it.

He hides the sun with a sieve.

He is a fool who cannot be angry, but he is a wise man who will not.

He is a fool that praises himself and a madman that speaks ill of himself.

He is a fool who buys an ox to have good cream.

He is building a bridge over the sea.

He is fool enough himself who will bray against another ass.

He is making clothes for fishes.

He is making ropes of sand.

He is not a wise man who cannot play the fool on occasion.

He looks for his ass and sits upon his back.

He seeks water in the sea.

He seeks wool on an ass.

He takes a spear to kill a fly.

He takes oil to extinguish the fire.

He that blows in the fire will get sparks in his eyes.

He that is a wise man by day is no fool by night.

He that makes himself an ass must not take it ill if men ride on him.

He that slanders is a fool.

He who is born a fool is never cured.

He who is of no use to himself is of no use to anyone.

He who won't be advised can't be helped.

He who would make a fool of himself will find many to help him.

Heaven protects children, sailors and drunken men.

If fools wore white caps we would seem a flock of geese.

If folly were a pain there would be groaning in every house.

If one, two, three say you are an ass then put on a bridle.

If the fool have a hump no one notices; if the wise man has a pimple everyone talks about it.

If there were no fools there would be no wise men.

If thou play the fool, stay for the fellow.

If we will have the kindness of others we must endure their follies.

If you want to get into the bog, ask five fools the way to the woods.

It is a cunning part to play the fool well.

It is better to associate with the half fool than with the half wise.

It is better to be saved with the fool than to perish with the wise.

It is better to please a fool than to anger him.

It is folly to drown on dry land.

It is folly to fear what we cannot avoid.

It is folly to sing twice to a deaf man.

It is well to profit by the folly of others.

It needs a cunning hand to shave a fool's head.

It's no use crying over spilt milk.

Knaves and fools divide the world.

Learned fools are the greatest of all fools.

Light minds are pleased with trifles.

Little minds like weak liquors are soonest soured.

Love of wit made no man rich.

Make your affairs known in the market place and one will call them black and another white.

Man learns to be wise by the folly of others.

Many that are wits in jest are fools in earnest.

Men may live fools, but fools they cannot die

Men talk wisely but live foolishly.

Mere wishes are silly fishes.

Mingle a little folly with your wisdom.

More people know Tom Fool than Tom Fool knows.

Much laughter, little wit.

Natural folly is bad enough, but learned folly is intolerable.

No creature smarts so little as a fool.

No fools so insufferable as those who affect to be wits.

No one is a fool always; everyone sometimes.

No show without punch.

Nobody is so wise but has a little folly to spare.

Nobody is twice a fool.

None but fiddlers and fools sing in front of their meat.

None but a fool distasteful truth will tell.

None is so wise but the fool overtakes him.

None so blind as those who won't see.

Nothing passes between asses but kicks.

Nothing so bold as a blind man.

Oftimes to please fools the wise men err.

One fool is enough in a house.

One fool praises another.

One should either be born a king or a fool.

Penny wise and pound foolish.

Praise a fool and you may make him useful.

Pride is the never failing vice of fools.

Proposing without performing is mere folly.

Send a fool to market and a fool he will return.

Silent fools may pass for wise.

Such as are careless of themselves can hardly be
mindful of others.

The ass does not know the worth of his tail until he
has lost it.

The ass eating oats dreams of thistles

The ass of a king is still but an ass.

The desire for the superfluous is folly for it hath no
bounds.

The false modesty of fools will conceal ulcers rather
than have them cured.

The fear of the Lord is the beginning of knowledge
but fools despise wisdom and instruction.

The feast passes and the fool remains.

The first day of April you may send a fool whither
you will.

The first degree of folly is to think one's self wise, the
next to tell others so, the third to despise all council.

The fish always stinks from the head downwards.

The follies of the fathers are no warning to the children.

The folly of one man is the fortune of another.

The fool cuts himself with his own knife.

The fool discerns the faults of others and forgets his own.

The fool doth think that he is wise, the wise man knows himself to be a fool.

The fool hunts for misfortune.

The fool runs away while his house is burning.

The fool speaks only folly.

The fool wanders, the wise man travels.

The fool wonders, the wise man asks.

The fool's pleasure costs him dear.

The foolish alchemist sought to make gold of iron and made iron of gold.

The greatest of all fools is he who is wise to soon.

The least foolish is accounted wise.

The malady that is most incurable is folly.

The more riches the fool hath, the greater fool he is.

The most exquisite folly is made of wisdom too tightly spun.

The older a fool the worse he is.

The praise of a fool is censure in disguise.

The shadow of a lord is the cap for a fool.

The shortest follies are the best.

The wise and the fool have their fellow.

The wise can learn of fools.

The wise make jests and the weak repeat them.

The wise man draws more advantage from his enemies than the fool from his friends.

The wise man when he holds his tongue says more than the fool when he speaks.

The wise must endure fools.

The wise seek wisdom, the fool has found it.

The wise too jealous are, fools too secure.

There are no foolish trades, there are only foolish people.

There is a fool at every feast.

There is no art can make a fool wise.

There is no fool like an old fool.

There is no knife cuts keener than a fool turned doctor.

There is no one so wise that wine does not make him a fool.

There is nothing blackens like the ink of fools.

There must be fools in the world.

They can do least who boast loudest.

Throw dirt enough and some will stick.

Throw not your axe so far you can't get it back.

To ask an elm tree for pears.

To be employed in useless things is to be half idle.

To counsel and disregard his own safety is folly.

To dig a well to put out a house on fire.

To dig a well with a needle.

To every fool his cap.

To promise and give nothing is comfort to a fool.

To reprove a fool is but lost labour.

To throw pearls before swine.

Trust not thy finger in a fool's mouth.

Truth and folly dwell in the wine cask.

Two fools in one house are too many.

Valiant fools were made by nature for the wise to work with.

We cannot all be wise.

We have all been fools in our time.

What is bred in the bone won't out in the flesh.

When a man becomes angry his reason rides out.

When the cat's away the mice will play.

When the moon is in the full, then the wit is in the wane

Where ignorance is bliss 'tis folly to be wise.

Where you see a jester a fool is not far off.

Who is in great haste should not ride an ass.

Whoever falls sick of folly is long in getting cured.

Whom the Gods would destroy, they first make mad.

Wine and women make fools of everybody.

Wise men change their minds, fools never.

Wise men have mouths in their hearts, fools their
hearts in their mouths.

Wise men learn from the mistakes of others, fools
from their own.

Wise men learn more from fools than fools learn from
wise men.

Wise men make proverbs and fools repeat them.

Wise men propose and fools determine.

Wishes can never fill the sack.

Wishes were ever fools.

Wishes won't wash dishes.

Wit and wisdom are rarely seen together.

Wit does not take the place of knowledge.

Wit is folly unless a wise man has the keeping of it.

Wit without wisdom cuts other men's meat and its own fingers.

Worthless is the advice of fools.

You can take a horse to water but you can't make him drink.

HEALTH AND HAPPINESS

A blithe heart makes a blooming visage.

A change is as good as a rest.

A cool mouth and warm feet live long.

A good heart overcomes evil fortune.

A good wife and health are a man's best wealth.

A happy heart is better than a full purse.

A happy life consists in virtue.

A joyous heart spins the hemp.

A man too busy to look after his health is like a mechanic too busy to look after his tools.

A merry fellow was never yet a sensible man.

A merry heart doth good like a medicine.

A merry host makes merry guests.

A pennyworth of mirth is worth a pound of sorrow.

All happiness is in the mind.

All our sweetest hours fly fastest.

All the joys in the world cannot take one grey hair out of our heads.

All who joy would win, must share it; happiness was born a twin.

Always merry is seldom rich.

An apple a day keeps the doctor away.

As he who has his health is young, so he who owes nothing is rich.

As long lives the merry heart as the sad.

Be always as merry as you can, foe no one delights in a sorrowful man.

Be happy when you can for you are a long time dead.

Be merry and wise.

Better lose a supper than have a hundred physicians.

By the side of sickness health becomes sweet.

Cheerful company shortens the miles.

Cheerfulness and goodwill make the labour light.

Cold hand, warm heart.

Content yourself with your own skin.

Continual cheerfulness is a sign of wisdom.

Do not jest if you cannot bear a jest.

Every life has its joy; every joy its law.

Everyone takes his pleasure where he finds it.

Feed a cold and starve a fever.

Good health is above wealth.

Happiness invites envy.

Happy he who can live in peace.

Happy he who can take warning from the mishap of others.

Happy is he that is content.

Happy is he that is happy in his children.

Happy is he that knows the folly of his youth.

Happy is he that serves the happy.

Happy is he whose friends were born before him.

Happy is the man who does all the good he talks of.

Happy is the man who keeps out of strife.

Happy men have happy friends.

Happy men have many friends.

He is happy who knows not himself to be otherwise.

He is happy who knows his good fortune.

He is not happy who knows it not.

He is truly happy who makes others happy.

He laughs best who laughs last.

He that goes to bed thirsty rises healthy.

He that is of merry heart hath a continual feast.

He that sits with his back to a draft sits with his face
to the coffin.

He who has not health has nothing.

He who is happy is rich enough.

He who laughs last laughs longest.

He who never was sick dies the first.

Health and cheerfulness mutually beget each other.

Health and understanding are the two great blessings of life.

Health is happiness.

Health is not valued till sickness comes.

Health is the vital principle of bliss.

If you can be well without health, you may be happy without virtue.

If your joys cannot be long, so neither can your sorrows.

In the time of mirth take heed.

It is a fortunate head that never ached.

It is a poor heart that never rejoices.

Joy and sorrow are next door neighbours.

Joy and sorrow usually succeed each other.

Joy is the tender shadow which sorrow casts.

Joy surfeited turns to sorrow.

Joy which we cannot share with others is only half enjoyed.

Joys are not the property of the rich alone.

Keep your feet dry and your head cool and for the rest live like a beast.

Laugh and the world laughs with you, weep and you weep alone.

Laughter is the best medicine.

Let them laugh that win.

Life is not mere existence but the enjoyment of health.

Living well is the best revenge we can take on our enemies.

Men go laughing to heaven.

Mirth and mischief are two things.

Mirth and motion prolong life.

Mirth cannot move a soul in agony.

Mirth is the medicine of life; it cures its ills and calms its strifes.

Neither gold nor grandeur can render us happy.

No cure, no pay.

No estate can make him rich that has a bad heart.

No happiness without holiness.

No joy like Heaven's.

No man can be called happy before his death.

No man can be happy without a friend, nor be sure of his friend till he is unhappy.

No man is happy unless he believes he is.

Not to wish to recover is a mortal symptom.

Obedience is the mother of happiness.

One hour of sleep before midnight is worth two after.

Spare diet and no trouble keep a man in good health.

Strong folks have strong maladies.

Study sickness while you are well.

Sudden joy kills sooner than excessive grief.

That is but slippery happiness that fortune can give and fortune can give away.

The best things in life are free.

The man that is happy in all things is more rare than the phoenix.

The memory of happiness makes misery woeful.

The more the merrier.

The wise with hope support the pains of life.

There is no happiness without virtue.

'Tis not good to be too happy too young.

'Tis only happiness can keep us young.

To be content with little is true happiness.

To be of use in the world is the only way to be happy.

To make one man happy you may calculate on making ten others miserable.

To rise at five, dine at nine, sup at five, go to bed at nine makes a man live to ninety- nine.

To the well man every day is a feast day.

True happiness is to no place confined, but still is found in a contented mind.

Variety is the spice of life.

Virtue and happiness are mother and daughter.

We are never so happy or fortunate as we think ourselves.

We are usually the best men when in the worst health.

We should publish our joys and conceal our griefs.

When joy is in the parlour, sorrow is in the passage.

When you are well keep as you are.

With mirth and laughter let the wrinkles come.

Without health life is not life, life is useless.

KNOWLEDGE AND LEARNING

A book that remains shut is but a block.

A book's a book though there is nothing in it.

A flow of words is no proof of wisdom.

A gem unwrought is a useless thing, so a man
  unlearned is a senseless being.

A golden key can open any door.

A good book praises itself.

A great book is a great evil.

A handful of good life is better than seven years of
  learning.

A learned man can only be appreciated by another
  learned man.

A library is a repository of medicine for the mind.

A little knowledge is a dangerous thing.

A man becomes learned by asking questions.

A man can know nothing of mankind without knowing something of himself.

A man cannot leave a better legacy to the world than a well educated family.

A man is not known until he comes to honour.

A man knows no more to any purpose than he practices.

A man profits more by the sight of an idiot than by the orations of the learned.

A man who is wise and learned, but without virtue, shall be despised.

A mind quite vacant is a mind quite distressed.

A profound thinker always thinks he is superficial.

A single conversation across the table with a wise man is better than ten years study of books.

A student usually has three maladies: poverty, itch and pride.

A teacher is better than two books.

A thinking man is always striking out something new.

A thousand probabilities do not make one truth.

A well prepared mind hopes in adversity, and fears in prosperity.

A wise man hath more ballast than sail.

A wise man is never less alone than when he is alone.

A word to the wise is enough.

Action is the proper fruit of knowledge.

Action must be founded on knowledge.

All is not true that is told.

All our knowledge is ourselves to know

All roads lead to Rome.

All we know is nothing is nothing can be known.

Art and knowledge bring bread and honour.

Art is long and life is short.

Be wisely worldly but not worldly wise.

Believe nothing of what you hear and half of what you see.

Better suffer for truth than prosper by falsehood.

Books are for company, the best friends and counsellors.

Books can never teach the use of books.

Books will speak plain when counsellors blanch.

Do not learn to do that from which there is no advantage.

Each one brings his understanding to market.

Education is the poor man's haven.

Education polishes good natures and corrects the bad ones.

Every good scholar is not a good schoolmaster.

Experience is the best teacher.

Experience is the father of wisdom.

Fact is stranger than fiction.

Facts are stubborn things.

Fine words butter no parsnips.

Genius is an infinite capacity for taking pains.

God deliver me from the man of one book.

Government of the will is better than increase of knowledge.

Great minds think alike.

Half our knowledge we must snatch, not take.

Half the world knows not how the other half lives.

Have thy study full of books rather than thy purse full of money.

He is sufficiently learned that knows how to do well, and has power enough to refrain from evil.

He is the happiest who knows nothing.

He knows enough who knows how to live and keep his own council.

He knows which side of his bread is buttered.

He teaches ill that teaches all.

He teaches me to be good that does me good.

He that follows truth too near will have dirt kicked in his face.

He that imagines he hath knowledge enough hath none.

He that knows himself knows others.

He that knows least commonly presumes most.

He that knows little soon repeats it.

He that teaches himself has a fool for a master.

He that would know what shall be must consider what hath been.

He that would learn to pray let him go to sea.

He who can, does, he who cannot, teaches.

He who has an art has everywhere a part.

He who has learned unlearns with difficulty.

He who increases knowledge increases sorrow.

He who knows but little tells it quickly.

He who knows himself best, esteems himself least.

He who knows little is confident in everything.

He who knows nothing never doubts.

He who thinks he knows most knows least.

He who understands most is other men's master.

Hidden knowledge differs little from ignorance.

History repeats itself.

I envy no man who knows more than myself but pity them that know less.

If thou love learning thou shalt be learned.

It is easy to be wise after the event.

It is for want of thinking that most men are undone.

It is good to learn at other men's cost.

It is never too late to learn.

It is not permitted to know all things.

It is not the quantity but the quality of knowledge that is valuable.

It is the mind that ennobles, not he blood.

It is the mind that makes the body rich.

It is vain to fish without a hook or learn to read without a book.

It is well for one to know more than he says.

It requires a long time to know anyone.

Know thyself.

Knowledge begins a gentleman but it is knowledge that completes him.

Knowledge comes but wisdom lingers.

Knowledge directs practice and practice increases knowledge.

Knowledge finds its price.

Knowledge is a second light and hath bright eyes.

Knowledge is a treasure but practice is the key to it.

Knowledge is folly, except grace guide it.

Knowledge is no burden.

Knowledge is power.

Knowledge is proud that he knows so much.

Knowledge is silver among the poor, gold among the nobles, and a jewel among princes.

Knowledge is the foundation of eloquence.

Knowledge makes one laugh but wealth makes one dance.

Knowledge must be gained by ourselves.

Knowledge without education is but armed injustice.

Knowledge without practice makes but half an artist.

Learn from your mistakes.

Learn not and know not.

Learn some useful art that you may be independent of the caprice of fortune.

Learn the luxury of doing good.

Learn to labour and wait.

Learning is a sceptre to some, a bauble to others.

Learning is an ornament in prosperity, a refuge in adversity, and a provision in old age.

Learning is better than house and land.

Learning is the eye of the mind.

Learning makes a good man better and a bad man worse..

Learning makes a man fit companion for himself.

Learning procures respect to good fortune and helps the bad.

Learning refines and elevates the mind.

Life without learning bears the stamp of death.

Little things please little minds.

Many a true word is spoken in jest.

Nature abhors a vacuum.

No book is so bad that something may be learned from it.

No man is so wise that he cannot become wiser.

No man knows until he hath tasted both fortunes.

No man learns but by pain or shame.

No man was ever wise by chance.

Not to know what has been transacted in former times is to continue always a child.

Nothing so much worth as a mind well educated.

One learns by failing.

One part of knowledge consists in being ignorant of such things as are not worthy of knowing.

One picture is worth a thousand words.

One should make a study of pastime.

Patience surpasses learning.

Practice makes perfect.

Profess not the knowledge thou hast not.

Say as men say, but think to yourself.

Science is organised knowledge.

Search all things, hold fast that which is true.

Seeing is believing.

Something is learned every time a book is opened.

Soon learnt, soon forgotten.

Study makes learned men but not always pious and
    wise.

Study to be useful

Take heed of many, the advice of few.

Take heed of the words of the wise.

Teaching others teaches yourself.

The best blood by learning is refined.

The exception proves the rule.

The first step to self-knowledge is self-distrust.

The fountain of wisdom flows through books.

The greatest learning is to be seen in the greatest plainness.

The intellect engages us in the pursuit of truth, the passions impel us to action.

The learned man has always riches in himself.

The least foolish is wise.

The meaning is best known to the speaker.

The mind is the man.

The more a man knows the more he is inclined to be modest.

The more understanding the fewer words.

The most learned are not the wisest.

The older one grows the more one learns.

The only jewel which will not decay is knowledge.

The pen is mightier than the sword.

The rust of the mind is the blight of genius.

The seeds of knowledge may be planted in solitude but must be cultivated in public.

The tutors of youth have an ascendancy over the stars of their nativity.

The wise man does not hang his knowledge on a hook.

There are two sides to every question.

There are two sides to every story.

There is always a first time.

There is more learning than knowledge in the world.

There is no education like adversity.

There is no royal road to learning.

Think much, speak little and write less.

Think with the wise but talk with the vulgar.

Thinking is not knowing.

Thinking is very far from knowing.

Through being too knowing the fox lost his tail.

To be conscious you are ignorant is a great step towards knowledge.

To know all is to forgive all.

To know how many beans make five.

To know one perfectly one must live in the same house as him.

To know one's self is true progress.

To know the disease is the commencement of the cure.

To know where the shoe pinches.

To know which way the wind blows.

Travel broadens the mind.

Truth lies at the bottom of a well.

Truth will out.

Two heads are better than one.

What you don't know can't hurt you.

When house and land are gone and spent, the learning is most excellent.

Where ignorance is bliss 'tis folly to be wise.

Who has never done thinking never begins doing.

Who knows forgives most.

Who knows most believes least.

Who teaches often learns himself.

Without knowledge there is no sin.

Word by word the great books are made.

You cannot teach your grandmother to suck eggs.

You may pay more for your schooling than your learning is worth.

Your knowing a thing is nothing unless another knows you know it.

Zeal without knowledge is fire without light.

LOVE AND MARRIAGE

A bonny bride is soon dressed.

A boy's love is water in the sieve.

A brilliant daughter makes a brittle wife.

A cold lover is a faithless friend.

A dark man is a jewel in a fair woman's eye.

A deaf husband and a blind wife are always a happy
couple.

A fence between makes love more keen.

A good Jack makes a good Jill.

A good son makes a good husband.

A good wife and health are a man's best wealth.

LOVE AND MARRIAGE

A good wife makes a good husband.

A great dowry is a bed full of brambles.

A growing moon and a flowing tide are lucky times to marry in.

A kiss of the mouth often touches not the heart.

A lover's soul lives in the soul of his mistress.

A maiden with many wooers often chooses the worst.

A man has a choice to begin love, but not to end it.

A man without a wife is a man without a care.

A man without a wife, a house without a roof.

A pretty face is half a dowry.

A rich bride goes young to the church.

A sweet and innocent compliance is the cement of love.

Absence makes the heart grow fonder.

Affinity in hearts is the nearest kindred.

All are fools or lovers first or last.

All mankind love a lover.

All's fair in love and war.

Always in love never married.

Always a bridesmaid, never a bride.

Among thorns grow roses.

An expensive wife makes a pensive husband.

An oyster may be crossed in love.

As is the lover so is the beloved.

Be loving and you will never want for love.

Beauties without fortune have sweethearts plenty but husbands none at all.

Better be an old man's darling than a young man's slave.

Better one house spoiled than two.

Cold cools the love that kindled too hot.

Deep lies the heart's language.

Esteem and love were never to be sold.

Every heart hath its own ache.

Every lover is a soldier.

Faint heart never won fair lady.

Fanned fire and forced love never did well yet.

Far from the eyes, far from the heart.

Fire in the heart sends smoke into the head.

Follow love and it will flee, flee love and it will
follow thee.

For love of the nurse many kiss the child.

For love the wolf eats the sheep.

For the lover, travel and patience.

For the sake of the knight, the lady kisses the squire.

Forced love does not last.

Generally we love ourselves more than we hate
others.

Glasses and lasses are brittle wares.

Gold and love affairs are hard to hide.

Hanging and wiving go by destiny.

Happy's the wooing that's not long in doing.

He loves thee well who makes thee weep.

He loves well who chastises well.

He loves well who never forgets.

He that has luck leads the bride to church.

He that hath love in his heart hath spurs in his heels.

He that is an enemy of the bride does not speak well
of the wedding.

He that will thrive must first ask the wife.

He who dances well goes from wedding to wedding.

He who takes a wife takes a master.

He who would not be indolent let him fall in love.

He who would the daughter win, with the mother
must begin.

Hearts alone buy hearts.

Hell hath no fury like a woman scorned.

Honey catches more flies than vinegar.

Honour in love is silence.

Hot love and hasty vengeance.

If you can kiss the mistress, never kiss the maid.

If you would be happy for a week take a wife.

It is best to be off with the old love before you are on with the new.

It is hard to wife and thrive both in the same year.

It is loving too much to die of love.

It takes two to tango.

Kissing goes by favour.

Let him not be a lover who has no courage.

Love abounds in honey and poison.

Love all, trust a few, be false to none.

Love and a cough cannot be hid.

Love and faith are seen in works.

Love and light cannot be hid.

Love and pride stalk bedlam.

Love asks faith and faith asks firmness.

Love begets love.

Love begins at home.

Love but laughs at lover's perjury.

Love can make any place look agreeable.

Love can neither be bought nor sold; its only price is love.

Love ceases to be a pleasure when it ceases to be a secret.

Love comes by looking.

Love comes in at the window and out by the door.

Love conquers all things, let us yield to love.

Love conquers all.

Love delights in praise.

Love does much, but money does more.

Love does wonders but money makes marriage.

Love expels jealousy.

Love fears no danger.

Love grows with obstacles.

Love has no law.

Love is a sweet tyrant because the lover endures his torments willingly.

Love is a thing full of anxious fears.

Love is as strong as death, jealousy as cruel as the grave.

Love is as strong as death, many waters cannot quench love, neither can the floods drown it.

Love is better than fame.

Love is blind.

Love is never without jealousy.

Love is not to be found in the market.

Love is the soul of genius.

Love is the touchstone of virtue.

Love is the wisdom of the fool and the folly of the wise.

Love is without prudence and anger without counsels.

Love knows hidden paths.

Love knows no measure.

Love laughs at locksmiths.

Love levels all inequalities.

Love lies in cottages as well as courts.

Love makes all hearts gentle.

Love makes labour light.

Love makes one fit for any work.

Love makes the world go round.

Love makes time pass away, and time makes love pass away.

Love must be attracted by beauty of mind and body.

Love rules his kingdom without a sword.

Love sees no faults.

Love sought is good, but given unsought is better.

Love teaches asses to dance.

Love warms more than a thousand fires.

Love will find the way.

Love without return is like a question without an answer.

Love yields no employment.

Love's anger is fuel to love.

Love's humility is love's pride.

Love's plant must be watered with tears and tended with care.

Love's the noblest frailty of the mind.

Love, knavery, and necessity make men good orators.

Love, thieves and fear make ghosts.

Lovers are fools.

Lovers break not hours unless to come before their time.

Lovers ever run before the clock.

Lovers live by love as larks live by leeks.

Lovers remember everything.

Lovers think others blind.

Lucky at cards, unlucky in love.

Man loves but once.

Marriage has it's pains, but a bachelor's life has no pleasures.

Marriage is a lottery.

Marriages are made in heaven.

Marry and grow tame.

Marry first and love will follow.

Marry in haste and repent in leisure.

Marry in lent, live to repent.

Marry in May, rue for aye.

Marry with your match.

Men are April when they woo, December when they wed.

Never choose your women or your linen by candlelight.

Never marry for money, but marry where money is.

New loves drive out the old.

No folly to being in love.

No God above gets all man's love.

No jealousy, no love.

No love without bread and wine.

No man is a match for a woman until he is married.

No rose without a thorn, no love without a rival.

None but the brave deserve the fair.

Old love does not rust.

Old lover, young fool.

One always returns to one's first love.

One cannot love and be wise.

One grows used to love and to fire.

One wedding brings another.

Out of the fullness of the heart love speaks.

Perfect love never settled in a high head.

Pity is akin to love.

Prettiness makes no pottage.

See for your love and buy for your money.

She that is born a beauty is half married.

She who loves an ugly man thinks him handsome.

The bravest are the tenderest, the loving are the
daring.

The conversation of lovers is inexhaustible.

The course of true love never did run smooth.

The faded rose no suitor knows.

The grey mare is the better horse.

The heart has its reasons, of which reason knows nothing.

The husband is always the last to know.

The lover in the husband may be lost.

The oaths of one that loves a woman are not to be believed.

The only victory over love is flight.

The prostrate lover when he lowest lies, but stoops to conquer, but kneels to rise.

The quarrel of lovers is the renewal of love.

The sight of lovers feed those in love.

The soul is not where it lives but where it loves.

The truth of truths is love.

The two greatest stimulants are love and debt.

The way to a man's heart is through his stomach.

The weeping bride makes a laughing wife.

There are as good fish in the sea as ever came out of it.

There are no reasons that explain love, but a thousand that explain marriage.

There goes more to marriage than four bare legs in a bed.

There is more pleasure in loving than in being loved.

There is no handsome woman on the wedding day except the bride.

'Tis better to have loved and lost than never to have loved at all.

To woo is a pleasure in young men, a fault in old.

Unkissed; unkind.

We never know how much we loved till what we loved was lost.

Wedlock is a padlock.

What comes from the heart goes to the heart.

When poverty comes in at the door, love flies out the window.

When two partners are of one mind, clay is into gold refined.

When you go to the dance take heed who you take by the hand.

Where there is great love there is great pain.

Where there is no love all faults are seen.

Where there is not equality there can be no perfect love.

Where we do not respect we soon cease to love.

Who would be loved must love.

Whom we love best to them we can say least.

Works and not words are the proof of love.

POVERTY AND WEALTH

A beggar can never be bankrupt.

A beggar is never out of his road.

A beggar's purse is bottomless.

A beggar's wallet empty is heavier than a full one.

A clown enriched knows neither relation or friend.

A fallen rich man may make a good master, but not an enriched poor man.

A great fortune is a great slavery.

A hungry man is an angry man.

A lamb is as dear to a poor man as an ox to the rich.

A light purse makes a heavy heart.

A little house well filled, a little land well tilled, and a little wife well willed are great riches.

A man that keeps riches and enjoys them not, is like an ass that carries gold and eats thistles.

A man who is proud of his money rarely has anything else to be proud of.

A man without money is like a bow without an arrow.

A man without money is like a ship without sails.

A miser grows rich by seeming poor, an extravagant man grows poor by seeming rich.

A moneyless man goes quick through the market.

A north wind has no corn and a poor man no friend.

A penny is sometimes better spent than spared.

A poor man has not many marks for fortune to shoot at.

A poor man is hungry after eating.

A poor man wants something, a covetous man all things.

A poor man's debt makes a great noise.

A poor man's joy has much alloy.

A poor man's shilling is but a penny.

A proud mind and a poor purse are ill met.

A proud pauper and a rich miser are contemptible things.

A ragged sack holds no grain, a poor man is not taken into counsel.

A rich child often sits in a poor mother's lap.

A rich man is either a rogue or a rogue's heir.

A rich man is never ugly in the eyes of a girl.

A rich man knows not his friends.

A rich man without understanding is a sheep with golden wool.

A rich man's foolish sayings pass for wise ones.

A rich mouthful, a heavy groan.

A thousand pounds and a bottle of hay are just the same at doomsday.

All ask if a man be rich, none if he be good.

All powerful money gives birth and beauty.

All strive to give to the rich man.

As long as there are some poorer than you, praise God even if you are unshod.

As water runs towards the shore, so does money towards the rich man's hand.

At the door of the rich are many friends, at the door of the poor none.

Bad money always comes back.

Be considerate towards the poor.

Before the rich man is willing to give, the poor man dies.

Beggars and borrowers cannot be choosers.

Better beg than steal.

Better die a beggar than live a beggar.

Better rich in God than rich in gold.

Blessed be nothing when the tax gatherer comes around.

But few prize money before honour.

Do not lend your money to a great man.

Don't borrow from a poor man.

Every one is kin to the rich man.

Every poor man is counted a fool.

Fair money can cover much that's foul.

For one rich man that is content there are a hundred
who are not.

For poor people, small coin.

Give and spend, and God will send.

Give me neither poverty or riches.

Giving much to the poor doth increase a man's store.

God help the poor for the rich can help themselves.

God help the poor, the rich can beg.

God helps them that help themselves.

God makes and apparel shapes, but it is money that
makes the man.

God sends us of our own when the rich men go to
dinner.

Hat in hand goes through the land.

Have you goods, have you none, lose heart and all is gone.

He alone is rich who makes proper use of his riches.

He bears poverty very ill who is ashamed of it.

He has riches enough who need neither borrow nor flatter.

He is not fit for riches who is afraid to use them.

He is not poor that hath not much, but he that craves much.

He is not rich who is not satisfied.

He is poor indeed that can promise nothing.

He is rich enough who does not want.

He is rich enough who has true friends.

He is rich enough who owes nothing.

He is richest who is content with least, for content is the wealth of a nation.

He is too poor to buy a rope to hang himself.

He is truly rich who desires nothing and he is truly poor who covets all.

He that does not save his pennies will never have pounds.

He that goes a borrowing goes a sorrowing.

He that goes barefoot must not plant thorns.

He that has nothing to spare must not keep a dog.

He that hath no money in his pot, let him have it in his mouth.

He that hath no money in his purse should have fair words on his lips.

He that hath no money shall need no purse.

He that hath nothing is not contented.

He that hath plenty of goods shall have more.

He that hath lost his credit is dead to the world.

He that hoards up money takes pains for other men.

He that is fallen cannot help him that is down.

He that is known to have no money has neither friends nor credit.

He that lies on the ground can fall no further.

He that makes haste to be rich, shall not be innocent.

He that never fails never grows rich.

He that shows his money shows his judgement.

He that wants money is accounted among those that want wit.

He that wants to be rich in a year comes to the gallows in half a year.

He that will not stoop for a pin shall never be worth a pound.

He who despises small things seldom grows rich.

He who devours the substance of the poor, will find at length a bone to choke him.

He who is rich can have no vice and he that is poor can have no virtue.

He who knows how to beg may leave his money at home.

He who pays the piper may call the tune.

He who stoppeth his ear at the cry of the poor, shall cry himself and not be heard.

He who throws away money with his hands, will seek it with his feet.

Health and money go far.

I never knew a silent rich man.

If money be not thy servant it will be thy master.

If poor, act with caution.

If rich be not elated, if poor be not dejected.

If riches were granted even beggars would become rich.

If you had as little money as manners you'd be the poorest of all your kin.

If you have money take your seat,
If you have none take to your feet.

If you make money your god, 'twill plague you like the devil.

Is it not sheer madness to live poor to die rich.

It is a miserable sight to see a poor man proud and a rich man avaricious.

It is a rare miracle for money to lack a master.

It is better to be poor and well than rich and ill.

It is better to be poor with honour than rich with shame.

191

It is not without a purpose when a rich man greets a poor man with kindness.

It would make a man scratch where he doth not itch to see a man live poor to die rich.

Men often seem rich to become rich.

Mention money and the world is silent.

Moderate riches will carry you, if you have more you must carry them.

Money amassed either serves or rules us.

Money answers all things.

Money borrowed is soon sorrowed.

Money burns many.

Money does all.

Money does not get hanged.

Money in purse will always be in fashion.

Money in whatever hands will confer power.

Money is a good servant but a bad master.

Money is a sword that can cut even the Gordian knot.

POVERTY AND WEALTH

Money is a universal language speaking any tongue.

Money is lost only for the want of money.

Money is money's brother.

Money is needed both by monk and dervish.

Money is power.

Money is the best bait to fish for man with.

Money is the fruit of evil as often as the root of it.

Money is the god of the world.

Money is the measure of all things.

Money is the only power that all mankind bow down before.

Money is the picklock that never fails.

Money is the root of all evil.

Money is the sinews of love as well as war.

Money is the soul of business.

Money is the very life and blood of mortals.

Money is wise, it knows it's own way.

Money lent, an enemy made.

Money makes dogs dance.

Money rules the world.

Money taken, freedom forsaken.

Money talks.

Money turns bad into good.

Money will make the pot boil though the devil pour water on the fire.

Money wins the battle, not the long arm.

Much wisdom is lost in poor men's mouths.

Much wisdom is smothered in a poor man's head.

Much wit is lost in a poor man's purse.

My money is little, my heart without strife.

Need conquers pride.

Neither a borrower nor a lender be.

No good man ever becomes suddenly rich.

No one is poor but he who thinks himself so.

No one so hard upon the poor as the pauper who has got into power.

No one so liberal as he who has nothing to give.

None have all and none have nothing.

Not he who has little, but he who wishes for more is poor.

Not possession but use is the only riches.

Nothing have, nothing crave.

Once poor, my friend, still poor you must remain, The rich alone have all the means of gain.

One day a beggar the next a thief.

One never gets more than the money's worth of anything.

Poor and content is rich and rich enough.

Poor folk's wisdom goes for little.

Poor folks say "thank you" for a little.

Poor men do penance for rich men's sins.

Poor men seek meat for their stomachs, rich men stomachs for their meat.

Poor men's tables are soon spread.

Poor men's words have little weight.

Poor without debt is better than a prince.

Poor, what he can; rich, what he will.

Poor men's money and cowards' weapons are often flourished.

Poverty is a good all men hate.

Poverty is no sin, but it is terribly inconvenient.

Poverty makes a man mean.

Pride breakfasted with plenty, dined with poverty, supped with infamy.

Public money is like holy water; everyone helps himself to it.

Put not your trust in money but your money in trust.

Rather a man without money, than money without a man.

Rather be a hog than an ignorant rich man.

Rich for yourself, poor for your friend.

Rich in gold, rich in care.

Rich men and fortunate men have need of much prudence.

Rich men are slaves condemned to the mines.

Rich men feel misfortunes that pass over poor men's heads.

Rich men have no faults.

Rich men seem happy, great and wise, all which the good man only is.

Rich men's spots are covered with money.

Rich people are everywhere at home.

Riches abuse them who know not how to use them.

Riches and cares are inseparable.

Riches and favour go before wisdom and art.

Riches and virtue do not always keep each other company.

Riches are always restless; it is only to poverty the gods give content.

Riches are but the baggage of fortune.

Riches are first to be sought for, after wealth virtue.

Riches are like muck which stinks in a heap but spread abroad makes the earth fruitful.

Riches are often abused but never refused.

Riches breed care, poverty is safe.

Riches cause arrogance, poverty meekness.

Riches come better after poverty than poverty after riches.

Riches hath made more men covetous, than covetousness hath made men rich.

Riches hath their embarrassments.

Riches have wings.

Riches never come even by chance to him whose destiny it is to be poor.

Riches only adorn the house, but virtue adorns the person.

Riches serve the wise man but command the fool.

Riches take peace from the soul but rarely if ever confer it.

Riches well got and well used are a blessing.

Riches will bear out folly.

Riches without understanding, a body without a soul.

Take care of the pennies and the pounds will look after themselves.

That costs dear which is bought with begging.

That man is not poor who has the use of things necessary.

That which is stamped a penny will never be a pound.

The abuse of riches is worse than the want of them.

The art is not in making money but in keeping it.

The cottage is a palace to the poor.

The dainties of the great are the tears of the poor.

The devil wipes his tail with the poor man's pride.

The foolish saying of the rich man pass laws in society.

The impartial earth is open to the poor as well as the sons of kings.

The miser and the pig are of no use till dead.

The miser is always poor.

The money paid, the work delayed.

The money you refuse will never do you good.

The only good a miser does is to prove the little happiness there is to be found in wealth.

The pleasures of the mighty are the terrors of the poor.

The poor are rich when they are satisfied.

The poor can live in one house together when two kings cannot in a kingdom.

The poor cannot, the rich will not.

The poor is always put to the worst.

The poor live secure.

The poor man eats at double cost.

The poor man must keep his word, and the rich when it suits him.

The poor man seeks for food, the rich man for appetite.

The poor man turns his cake and another comes and takes it away.

The poor man wants much, the miser everything.

The poor man's budget is full of schemes.

The poor man's coin always grows thin.

The poor man's honour is worth more than the rich man's gold.

The poor man's penny unjustly obtained is a coal of fire in the rich man's purse.

The poor man's wisdom is as useless as a palace in the wilderness.

The poor must dance as the rich pipe.

The poor pay for all.

The poor pour, and the rich drink the wine.

The poor rich man is emphatically poor.

The poor sing free throughout the world.

The poor sit in Paradise on the first benches.

The poor trying to imitate the powerful perish.

The poor you always have with you.

The poorhouses are filled with the most honest people.

The pride of the rich makes the labours of the poor.

The rich are trustees under God for the poor.

The rich can only eat with one mouth.

The rich man carries nothing away with him but his shroud.

The rich man is often poorer than the beggar.

The rich need not beg a welcome.

The rich never need for kindred.

The rich rule over the poor and the borrower is servant to the lender.

The rich think poor men have no souls.

The riches of the miser fall into the hands of the spendthrift.

The sign invites you but your money must get you out.

The smell of money is good, come whence it may.

The thirst for money brings all the sins into the world.

The whole world is the house of the rich and they may live in whatever apartment they please.

The wise discourses of a poor man go for nothing.

The wolf is sometimes satisfied, the miser never.

There are many things that may not be uttered by men in threadbare coats.

There are none so poor they cannot help, and none so rich as not to need help.

There be as many miseries beyond riches as on this side of them.

There is God's poor and the devil's poor, the first from providence, the other from vice.

There is no revenging yourself on a rich man.

Those who believe money can do everything are frequently prepared to do everything for money.

To be rich one must have a relation at home with the devil.

To beg of the miser is to dig a hole in the sea.

To condemn the poor because of their poverty is to affront God's providence.

To disregard money on suitable occasions is often a great profit.

To have nothing is to have rich eyes and poor hands.

Touch not another man's money, for the most honest never added to it.

We give the rich, and take from the poor.

What the poor are to the poor none knows but themselves and God.

When honour grew mercenary, money grew honourable.

When money speaks, truth keeps silent.

When riches increase , the body decreases.

When the poor become rich they sink the village.

Where nothing is nothing can be had.

Where there's money there's the devil, But where there's none a greater evil.

Where there's muck, there's money.

Wherever a poor man is, there is his destiny.

Who closes his ear to the poor, Peter will not hear when he knocks.

Who has nothing fears nothing.

Who is not ashamed to beg is soon not ashamed to steal.

Who is wealthy and free is rich.

Who nothing have shall nothing save.

Who readily borrows, readily lies.

Who will become rich must cast his soul behind the money-chest.

Who will become rich must have great care and little conscience.

With money you would not know yourself, without money nobody would know you.

Withhold not the wages of the poor.

Without money, without fear.

Would you know the value of money go borrow some.

You will see more ruined than saved by ill-gotten money.

POWER AND CONFLICT

A brave man will yield to a brave man.

A brave man's country is wherever he chooses his abode.

A bully is always a coward.

A cake eaten in peace is worth two in trouble.

A cat may look at a King.

A certain peace is to be preferred to an expected victory.

A chain is no stronger than it's weakest link.

A crown is no cure for the headache.

A foreign war is preferable to one at home.

A gallant man needs no drums to rouse him.

A good cause makes a stout heart and a strong arm.

A good prince does not cut out freedom's tongue.

A house divided against itself cannot stand.

A king is never powerful that hath not power on the sea.

A patriot is a fool in any age.

A poor freedom is better than a rich slavery.

A proud soldier is fellow to the king.

A short sword for a brave man.

A stick is a peacemaker.

A tyrant's breath is another's death.

A war, even when most victorious, is a national misfortune.

Absolute power corrupts absolutely.

All are brave when the enemy flies.

All are not free who mock their chains.

All are not princes that ride with the emperor.

All men can't be masters.

Ambition is the last infirmity of noble minds.

Ambition is the soldier's virtue.

Ambition is torment enough for an enemy.

Ambition knows no gorge but the grave.

An ill man in office is a mischief to the public.

An office that does not give the holder enough to eat
is not worth two beans.

An oppressive government is more to be feared than a
tiger.

Argument makes three enemies to one friend.

Argument seldom convinces anyone against their
inclination.

As princes fiddle, subjects must dance.

At the wars do as they do at the wars.

Attack is the best form of defence.

Before the time great courage, when at the point great
fear.

Better a lean peace than a fat victory.

Better a master be feared than despised.

Better be a free bird than a captive king.

Better free in a foreign land than a slave at home.

Big fish eat little fish.

Black ambition stains a public cause.

Blood will have blood.

Bribes will enter without knocking.

By wisdom peace, by peace plenty.

Common-sense is the growth of all countries.

Conspiracies no sooner should be formed than executed.

Corporations have neither bodies to be punished, nor souls to be damned.

Councils of war never fight.

Courage in danger is half the battle.

Courage in war is safer than cowardice.

Courage, conduct and perseverance conquer all before them.

Cursed is he that doth his office craftily, corruptly or maliciously.

Diamonds cut diamonds.

Divide and rule.

Do as would be done by.

Dog does not eat dog.

Eagles don't catch flies.

Even the worm will turn

Even war is better than a wretched peace.

Every dog will have its day.

Every man for himself.

Every man has his price.

Every man is master in his own house.

Every one has his master.

Everybody loves a lord.

Everyone is emperor on his own ground.

Fight fire with fire.

Forewarned is forearmed.

From prudence peace, from peace abundance.

Give me liberty or give me death.

Good fences make good neighbours.

Good kings never make war but for the sake of peace.

Great office, great care.

Happy is the country that has no history.

He hath a great office, he must need thrive.

He is most powerful that governs himself.

He must be strong indeed who takes the club from
  Hercules.

He that commands well shall be obeyed well.

He that hath a fellow ruler hath an over-ruler.

He that is hated by his subjects cannot be king.

He that makes a good war makes a good peace.

He that makes himself a sheep shall be eaten by the
  wolf.

He that put on a public gown must put off the private
  person.

He that stands may fall.

He that will out wit the fox must rise before him.

He who cannot command himself, it is folly to think to command others.

He who demands does not command.

He who fights and runs away may live to fight another day.

He who has land hath war.

He who pays the piper may call the tune.

He who stands high is seen from afar.

He who would rule, must hear and be deaf, see and be blind.

If peace cannot be maintained with honour it is no longer peace.

If you can't beat them, join them.

If you can't stand the heat, get out of the kitchen.

Impartial vigour and example are the best means of governing.

In a false quarrel there is no true valour.

In the land of the blind the one-eyed man is king

In time of war the devil makes more room in hell.

In war according to war.

In war reputation is strength.

It is a bad war from which no one returns.

It is much safer to obey than rule.

It is skill not strength that governs a ship.

It is the raised stick makes the dog obey.

It is thou must honour the office and not the office thee.

It takes two to make a quarrel.

Kings love the treason, but not the traitor.

Kings ought to be kings in all things.

Little is done where many command.

Mad wars destroy in one year the works of many years of peace.

Many are called but few are chosen.

Many return from the war who cannot give an account of the battle.

213

Might is right.

Money is power.

New brooms sweep clean.

No affections and a great brain; these are the men to
command the world.

No government can be long secure without a
formidable opposition.

No man can serve two masters.

No office so humble but is better than nothing.

No one can have peace longer than his neighbour
pleases.

No prince is poor that hath rich subjects.

No ruler good save God.

Of a master who never forgives, the orders are
seldom disobeyed.

Of all wars peace ought to be the end.

Office tests the man.

Office without pay makes thieves.

Old politicians chew on wisdom past.

One hand washes the other.

One man with courage makes a majority.

One man's loss is another man's gain.

One peace is better than ten victories.

One sword keeps another in the scabbard.

One volunteer is worth two pressed men.

Only one can be emperor.

Oppression causes rebellion.

Oppression will make a wise man mad.

Our master is our enemy.

Peace flourishes when reason rules.

Peace in the village is better than war in the city.

Peace is the father of friendship.

Peace with a cudgel in hand is war.

Peace without truth is poison.

Power goes before talent.

Power on my head or the raven on my corpse.

Power tends to corrupt, and absolute power corrupts absolutely.

Power weakens the wicked.

Rebellion to tyrants is obedience to God.

Reform that you may prosper.

Rewards and punishment are the basis of a good government.

See, listen, and be silent, and you will live in peace.

Set thine house in order.

Small strokes fell great oaks.

Such is the government, such is the people

Talk of the war but do not go to it.

The ballot is stronger than the bullet.

The best government is that which governs least

The bigger they are the harder they fall.

The cause finds arms.

The choice of the people is the surest and best title to reign over them.

The fear of war is worse than the war itself.

The first duty of a soldier is obedience.

The greatest king must at last go to bed with a shovel.

The greatest of all evils is a weak government.

The hearts of the people are the only legitimate
foundations of empire.

The king can do no wrong.

The king's favour is no inheritance.

The mob has many heads but no brains.

The office shows the man.

The race is not to the swift, nor the battle to the
strong.

The right divine to govern wrong.

The subjects' love is the king's best guard.

The surest way to avoid a war is not to fear it.

The sword keeps the peace of the land.

The time of the prince belongs to the people.

The trap to the high born is ambition.

The tree of liberty grows only when watered by the blood of tyrants.

The unbought loyalty of men is the cheap defence of nations.

The voice of the people is the voice of God.

The weakest go to the wall.

The word of a king ought to be as binding as the oath of a subject.

The world without peace is the soldier's pay.

There are no miracles in politics.

There is a great force hidden in a sweet command.

There is no little enemy.

There is no worse heresy than that the office sanctifies the holder.

There is nothing humbler than ambition when it is about to climb.

There was never a good war nor a bad peace.

They conquer who believe they can.

They that buy an office must sell something.

They that govern most make least noise.

Those who cannot govern themselves must be governed.

'Tis sweet to die for one's country.

To command many will cost much.

To grow proud in office is the nature of man.

To preserve friendship one must build walls.

To take ambition from a soldier is to rob him of his spurs.

To the victor the spoils.

Troy was not taken in a day.

Two captains sink the ship.

Tyranny is far the worst treason.

United we stand, divided we fall.

War gives no opportunity for repeating a mistake.

War is a proceeding that ruins those who succeed.

War makes robbers and peace hangs them.

What belongs to the master is forbidden to the slave.

When all you have is a hammer everything looks like a nail.

When Greek meets Greek then comes the tug of war.

When power puts in its plea the laws are silent.

When the helm is gone the ship will soon be wrecked.

When the ship is sunk everyone knows she might have been saved.

When two play one must lose.

When war is raging the laws are dumb.

Where money and counsel are wanting it is better not to make war.

Where the cause is just the small conquers the great.

Who builds on the mob builds on sand.

Who fills an office must learn to bear reproach and blame.

Who loves peace serves God.

Who obtains an office surreptitiously like a wolf will administer it like a fox.

Who shall keep the keepers?

Whosoever draws his sword against the prince must throw the scabbard away.

Why keep a dog and bark yourself.

Without a shepherd sheep are not a flock.

You must ask your neighbour if you shall live in peace.

You must not be more royalist than the King.

PRUDENCE, CAUTION AND EXCESS

A barley-corn is better than a diamond to a cockerel.

A belly full of gluttony will never study willingly.

A bird in the hand is worth two in the bush.

A bird never flew on one wing.

A bit in the morning is better than nothing all day.

A burnt child fears fire.

A closed mouth catches no flies.

A coconut shell full of water is an ocean to an ant.

A covetous man is good to none, but worse to himself.

A covetous man makes a halfpenny of a farthing and a liberal man makes sixpence of it.

A covetous man makes no friend.

A danger foreseen is half avoided.

A fine cage won't feed the bird.

A full belly neither fights nor flies well.

A glutton is never generous.

A good "take heed" will surely speed.

A grain of prudence is worth a pound of craft.

A jest driven too far often brings home hate.

A little pot is soon hot.

A little too late is much too late.

A man cannot whistle and drink at the same time.

A man never appreciates ashes until he slips on the ice.

A man of pleasure is a man of grief.

A miss is as good as a mile.

A modest dog seldom grows fat.

A nod is as good as a wink to a blind horse.

A penny saved is a penny got.

A place for everything and everything in it's place.

A promise is a debt.

A prudent haste is wisdom's leisure.

A prudent man does not make the goat his gardener.

A prudent man procures in summer the sleigh and in winter the wagon.

A prudent question is one half of wisdom.

A short cut is often a losing cut.

A stitch in time saves nine.

A watched pot never boils.

Abstinence and fasting cure many a complaint.

Abstinence is the best medicine.

Abstinence is the mother of competence.

Abundance begets indifference.

After one that earns comes one that wastes.

All comes right to him that can wait.

All covet, all lose.

All things belong to the prudent.

Always rise from the table with an appetite and you
will never sit down without one.

Always to be sparing is always to be in want.

Anyone who has to ask the cost cannot afford it.

At an auction keep your mouth shut.

Be just before you are generous.

Be slow in choosing, but slower in changing.

Better a good cow than a cow of good kind.

Better be envied than pitied.

Better gain in mud than lose in gold.

Better late than never.

Better on a sound boat than a leaky ship.

Better poor on land than rich at sea.

Better return half way than lose yourself.

Better safe than sorry.

Better sit still than rise up and fall.

Better spare at the brim than at the bottom.

Better spared than ill spent.

Better the devil you know than the devil you know not.

Better three hours too soon than a minute too late.

Better to be convinced by words than by blows.

Better twice measured than once wrong.

Big mouthfuls often choke.

Burning the candle at both ends.

Cast no dirt in the well that gives you water.

Colts by falling and lads by losing grow prudent.

Covet nothing over much.

Covetous men are neither clothed, fed nor respected.

Covetous men live drudges to die wretches.

Covetousness as well as prodigality brings a man to a morsel of bread.

Covetousness brings nothing home.

Covetousness is never satisfied until its mouth is full of dirt.

Covetousness is the father of unsatisfied desires.

Covetousness starves other vices.

Curiosity killed the cat.

Cut your coat according to your cloth.

Delays are dangerous.

Desires are nourished by delays.

Different strokes for different folks.

Dig a well before you are thirsty.

Do not cry out before you are hurt.

Do not give your measure to anyone but your tailor.

Do not go from one extreme to the other.

Do not hang all on one nail.

Do not meet troubles halfway.

Do not pass sentence before hearing the evidence.

Do not run too fast after gain.

Do not sail too near to the wind.

Do not strip before bedtime.

Do not take hold of a nettle, but if you do grasp it
tight.

Do not wade where you cannot see the bottom.

Don't believe in the saint unless he works miracles.

Don't build castles in the air.

Don't climb the hill until you get to it.

Don't count your chickens before they are hatched.

Don't cry herrings till they are in the net.

Don't curse the crocodile's mother before you cross the river.

Don't cut off your nose to spite your face.

Don't fly until your wings are feathered.

Don't go near the water until you have learned to swim.

Don't halloo until you are out of the woods.

Don't leave the high road for a short cut.

Don't put all your eggs in one basket.

Don't put your finger in too tight a ring.

Don't sell the bearskin until you have killed the bear.

Don't sing your triumph before you have conquered.

Don't snap you fingers at the dog before you are out
of the village.

Don't spoil the ship for a halfpenny worth of tar

Don't throw away your old shoes until you have got
new ones.

Don't throw out the baby with the bath-water

Don't throw out your dirty water until you have got
clean.

Drive gently over the stones.

Each person for his own skin.

Easy does it.

Enough is a feast, too much vanity.

Enough is as good as a feast to one that is not a beast.

Enough is as good as a feast.

Enough is better than a sack full.

Enough to keep the wolf from the door.

Every excess becomes a vice.

Every man draws the water to his own mill.

Every sparrow to its ear of wheat.

Everyone is bound to live within their means.

Everyone rakes the fire under his own pot.

Everything in excess is adverse to nature.

Excess of wine neither keeps secrets nor performs promises.

Extremes meet.

Fair and softly goes the day.

Fire is a good servant but a bad master.

First things first.

Frugality is a great revenue.

Frugality when all is spent comes too late.

Full bottles and glasses make swearers and asses.

Give and take is fair play.

Go further and fare worse.

Go to bed without supper and you will rise without debt.

Good at a distance is better than evil at hand.

Good and quickly seldom meet.

Good weight and measure is Heaven's treasure.

Good-nature without prudence is foolishness.

Govern your passions, otherwise they will govern you.

Grasp no more than thy hand will hold.

Greed and the eye can no man fill.

Greedy folks have long arms.

Gut no fish before you catch them.

Haste makes waste.

Haste often brings shame.

Hasty climbers have sudden falls.

He is the nearest to God that has the fewest wants.

He that desires but little has no need of much.

He that gets forgets, but he that wants thinks on.

He that grasps at all loses all.

He that runs in the dark may well stumble.

He that spares something today will have something to spare tomorrow.

He that has a glass roof should not throw stones at his neighbours.

He that is hasty fishes in an empty pond.

He that sows thorns shall never reap grapes.

He who spends more than he should, shall not have to spare when he would.

Health consists with temperance alone.

His eye is bigger than his belly.

Hurry no man's cattle.

If it is not broken, don't fix it.

If men will have no care for the future, they will soon have sorrow for the present.

If you can't be good, be careful.

If you play with fire expect to get burned.

If you pursue two hares both will get away from you.

If you would be well served, serve yourself.

It is an ill wind that blows nobody good.

It is best to be on the safe side.

It is hard to both have and want.

It is ill speaking between a full man and a fasting.

It is safest sailing within reach of the shore.

It is the last straw that breaks the camel's back.

It is the principle rule of life not to be too much
addicted to one thing.

It is too late to spare when the pocket is bare.

It is too late too shut the stable door after the horse
has bolted.

Keep a thing seven years and you will always find a
use for it.

Keep no more cats than will catch mice.

Keep the common road and thou art safe.

Keep the feast to feast to feast day.

Least said is soonest mended.

Less is more.

Let sleeping dogs lie.

Let well alone.

Let your purse be your master.

Live not to eat but eat to live.

Live within your harvest.

Look before you leap.

Make a virtue of necessity.

Make it do, or do without.

Measure a thousand times and cut once.

Measure is a merry mean.

Measure is a treasure.

Meat and mass never hindered man.

Milk the cow but don't pull off the udder.

Moderate measures succeed best.

Moderation in all things.

More men are drowned in the bowl than in the sea.

More than enough is too much.

More than we use is more than we want.

Much meat, much maladies.

Much on earth, but little in heaven.

Much would have more.

Necessity seeks bread where it is to be found.

Never answer a question until it is asked.

Never mention rope in the house of a man who has
   been hanged.

Nothing to excess.

Of two evils choose the less.

Once bitten, twice shy.

One hand for oneself and another for the ship.

One man's meat is another man's poison.

One pin for your mouth and two for your purse.

One step at a time.

Penny wise and pound foolish.

People who live in glass houses should not throw
   stones.

Please your eye and plague your heart.

Praise the sea but keep on land.

Produce much, consume little, labour diligently, speak cautiously.

Prudence supplies the want of every good.

Puff not against the wind.

Pull down your hat on the weak side.

Pull gently at a weak rope.

Regulate thy own passions and bear those of others.

Rule lust, temper the tongue, and bridle the belly.

Scatter with one hand gather with two.

Self is the first object of charity.

Self preservation is the first law of nature.

Send not to market for trouble.

Set your sail according to the wind.

Slowly but surely.

Softly, softly, catchee monkey.

Spare well and have to spend.

Spare your breath to cool your pottage.

Stretch your arm no further than your sleeve will reach.

Stretch your legs according to your coverlet.

Sweep before your own door.

Take care of the pence and the pounds will take care of themselves.

Take it easy and live long are brothers.

Take the middle of the way and thou wilt not fall.

The beaten road is the safest.

The bounty of nature is too little for the greedy man.

The gentle calf sucks all the cows.

The half is better than the whole.

The last drop makes the cup run over.

The less said the better.

The more a man denies himself, the more will he receive from heaven.

The more you get the more you want.

The more you stir the more it stinks.

The most prudent yield to the strongest.

The noblest task is to command one's self.

The pitcher will go to the well once too often.

The prudent still have fortune on their side.

The road to hell is paved with good intentions.

The table robs more than the thief.

There is always some trouble mixed up with the greatest pleasure.

There is many a slip 'twixt the cup and the lip.

There is safety in numbers.

Thousands drink themselves to death before one dies of thirst.

Three removes are as bad as a fire.

Thrift is a great revenue.

Too many sacks are the death of the ass.

Too much bed makes a dull head.

Too much of a good thing is a bad thing.

Too much water drowned the miller.

Too much wax burns the church.

Try before you trust.

Try the ice before you venture on it.

Two captains sink the ship.

Two watermelons cannot be held under one arm.

Waste not, want not.

What is done hastily is not done well.

What is enough is never little.

What is got over the devil's back is spent under his
belly.

What the eye doesn't see the heart doesn't grieve
over.

What you have, hold.

What you've never had you never miss.

What's done cannot be undone.

When all is consumed repentance comes too late.

Where necessity pinches, boldness is prudence.

Who hastens too much often leaves behind.

Who sows thorns should not go barefoot.

Whose carriage is greediness, his companion is
   beggary.

Wilful waste makes woeful want.

You can have too much of a good thing.

You cannot run with the hare and hunt with the
   hounds.

You cannot sail as you would but as the wind blows.

You must learn to walk before you can run.

You must shift your sail with the wind.

TIME, SEASON
AND WEATHER

A bad day never had a good night.

A bolt does not always fall when it thunders.

A bushel of March dust on the leaves is worth a king's ransom.

A cherry year, a merry year, a plumb year, a dumb year.

A cold April bread and wine.

A cold April the barn will fill.

A day to come shows longer than a year that's gone.

A dripping June sets all in tune.

A flow will have an ebb.

A foul morn may turn to a fine day.

A green Yule means a fat churchyard.

A hundred years hence we shall all be bald.

A hundred years is not much but never is a long time.

A red sky at night, shepherd's delight,
A red sky at morning, shepherd's warning.

A snow year is a rich year.

A thousand years hence the river shall run as it did.

A wet August never brings dearth.

A windy March and a rainy April, make a beautiful
May.

A swarm in May is worth a load of hay, a swarm in
June is worth a silver spoon, but a swarm in July is
not worth a fly.

After a storm comes the calm.

After clouds a clear sun.

After winter spring will come.

All good things must come to an end.

All the months in the year curse a fair February.

All the treasures of the earth would not bring back one lost moment.

All times when old are good.

All's well that ends well.

An evening red and a morning grey, is a sign of a fine day.

April and May are the key to the year.

April cling good for nothing.

April flood carries away the frog and her brood.

April showers bring forth May flowers.

As good have no time as make no good use of it.

As the day lengthens so the cold strengthens.

Calm weather in June sets corn in tune.

Coming events cast their shadow before.

Each day is the scholar of yesterday.

Each passing year robs us of something.

Enjoy today for tomorrow the first grey hair may come.

Every day brings a new light.

Every day hath its night, every weal its woe.

Every day in thy life is a day in thy history.

Every day is not a holiday.

Every scrap of a wise man's time is worth saving.

Every tomorrow brings its bread.

Everything has a time.

Everything has its time and that time must be watched.

Everything is of every year.

Everything may be bought except day and night.

Fair weather cometh out of the north.

February makes a bridge and March breaks it.

From tomorrow to tomorrow time goes a long journey.

He never broke his hour who kept his day.

He that has most time has none to lose.

He that has time and looks for more, loses time.

He that passes a winter's day escapes his enemy.

He who falls today may rise tomorrow.

He who gains time gains everything.

Hope springs eternal.

Hour by hour time departs.

If Candlemass day be sunny and bright, winter will have another flight; if Candlemass day be cloudy with rain, winter is gone and won't come again.

If in February there be no rain, neither good for hay nor rain.

If St. Paul's day be fair and clear, it will betide a happy year.

If the weather is fine put on your cloak; if it rains do as you please.

If things look badly today, they may look better tomorrow.

If today will not, tomorrow may.

In the wane of the moon a cloudy morning bodes a fair afternoon.

In time the savage bull doth bear the yolk.

It is a long lane that has no turning.

It is all one a hundred years hence.

It is easy to be wise after the event.

It is good to be in good time, you know not how long
it will last.

It is not spring until you can put you foot upon twelve
daisies.

It is time enough to set when the oven comes to the
dough.

It is time to yolk when the cart comes to the oxen.

It may be a fire but tomorrow it will be ashes.

It never thunders but it rains.

Lightning never strikes twice.

Long foretold, long last, short notice, soon past.

Lost time is never found again, and what we call time
enough always proves little enough.

Make hay while the sun shines.

Make the night night, and the day day, and you will
live pleasantly.

Man cannot buy time.

Many seek good nights and lose good days.

March borrows three days of April and they will be ill.

March comes in like a lion and out like a lamb.

March grass never did good.

March wind and May sun makes clothes white and maids dun.

March winds and April showers bring forth May flowers.

May borrows ten days from March to kill off cattle and old people.

May chickens come cheeping.

Never defer to tomorrow that which you can do today.

Never is a long time.

Never mind the weather, so the wind don't blow.

No day but has its evening.

No day is wholly productive of evil.

No day should pass without something being done.

No man can call back yesterday.

No man can tether time nor tide.

No time like the present.

No weather is ill, if the wind be still.

No-one has ever seen tomorrow.

No-one waits for yesterday.

On the first of March the crows begin to search.

Once in ten years a man hath need of another.

One hour today is worth two tomorrow.

One of these days is none of these days.

One swallow does not make a summer.

One today is worth two tomorrows.

One year borrows another year's food.

Open your door to a fine day, but make yourself
   ready for a foul one.

Other times, other folks.

Other times, other manners.

Praise a fine day at night.

Rain before seven, fine before eleven

Rain comes after sunshine, and after a dark cloud, a clear sky.

Saint Swithun's day, if thou be fair, for forty days it will remain; Saint Swithun's day, if thou bring rain, for forty days it will remain.

Seize the present day, giving no credit to the succeeding ones.

September blow soft, 'til the fruits in the loft.

So many mists in March, so many frosts in May.

Straw tells which way the wind blows.

Sufficient unto the day is the evil thereof.

Take time by the forelock.

Take time to be quick.

Take time when time is, for time will away.

The best preacher is time.

The better the day the better the deed.

The crutch of time does more than the club of Hercules.

DICTIONARY OF PROVERBS

The day has eyes, the night has ears.

The day is never so holy that the pot refuses to boil.

The day is short and the work is much.

The day sees the workmanship of the night and
laughs.

The day that you do a good thing there will be seven
new moons.

The days follow each other and are not alike.

The full moon brings fair weather.

The good time comes but once.

The greatest expense we can be at is that of our time.

The heavens are just, and time suppresses time.

The ill year comes in swimming.

The longest day must have an end.

The mill cannot grind with the water that is past.

The more snow the more healthy the season.

The past is for wisdom, the present for action, but for
joy the future.

TIME, SEASON AND WEATHER

The time to come is no more ours than the time past.

The sharper the storm the sooner it's over.

The sun loses nothing by shining into a puddle.

The year has a wide mouth and a big belly.

There is a time for all things.

There is a time to fish and a time to dry nets.

There is a time to jest and a time when jests are
   unreasonable.

There is no appeal from time past.

There is no better counsellor than time.

There is no day without its night.

There is no day without sorrow.

There is no hand to catch time.

There is nothing more precious than time.

There is nothing new under the sun.

Time and hour are not to be tied with a rope.

Time and hour run through the longest day.

Time at last sets all things even.

Time brings everything to those that can wait for it.

Time brings roses.

Time covers and discovers everything.

Time devours all things.

Time discovers everything.

Time dresses the greatest wounds.

Time enough is little enough.

Time fleeth away without delay.

Time heals all wounds.

Time is a file that wears and makes no noise.

Time is a river without banks.

Time is a true friend to sorrow.

Time is an unpaid advocate.

Time is anger's medicine.

Time is God's and ours.

Time is money.

Time is precious but truth is more precious than time.

Time is the great innovator.

Time is the herald of truth.

Time is the rider that breaks youth.

Time makes hay.

Time misspent is not lived but lost.

Time moves slowly to him whose employment it is to watch its flight.

Time passes like the wind.

Time past never returns, a moment lost is lost forever.

Time reveals all things.

Time rolls his ceaseless course.

Time stays not at he fool's leisure.

Time stoops to no man's lure.

Time subdues all things.

Time tries all.

Time works wonders.

Time, motion and wine cause sleep.

Times change and me with time.

To a child all weather is cold.

To him that does everything in its proper time one
day is worth three.

To save time is to lengthen life.

Today is yesterday's pupil.

Today must borrow nothing of tomorrow.

Today's egg is better than tomorrow's hen.

Tomorrow is another day.

Tomorrow never comes.

Tomorrow is fresh fields and pastures new.

Tomorrow never comes.

Tomorrow's remedy will not ward off the evil of
today.

Tomorrow's sun to thee may never rise.

Use not today what tomorrow may want.

We take no note of time but from its loss.

TIME, SEASON AND WEATHER

What a day may bring a day may take away.

What greater crime than loss of time.

What is my turn today, may be thine tomorrow.

What is new cannot be true.

What is wrong today won't be right tomorrow.

What lay hidden under the snow cometh to light at last.

What reason and endeavour cannot bring about time often will.

What will be will be.

What's done cannot be undone.

When it rains in August it rains honey and wine.

When it rains in February it will be temperate all the year.

Who has no time yet waits for time, comes to a time of repentance.

Winter eats what summer provides.

Winter finds out what summer lays up.

Winter is summer's heir.

255

Winter never rots in the sky.

Winter thunder makes summer wonder.

Years and sins are always more than owned.

You saddle today and ride out tomorrow.